ONE of the great graphic artists of the 19th century in France, Gustave Doré (1832-1883) is beginning to come into his own again. Several of his brilliantly illustrated books have recently been brought back into print, and now with this new edition of *The History of Holy Russia* we see how original and important he was—influencing artists all the way from Courbet (who once said, "There are only two of us!") to the popular David Levine of our own day.

Doré's famous illustrations to the Bible and to Dante, his sketches of London and Paris, have long been favorites among those who love an artist who has both a soaring imagination and a keen satirical eye for all the details of life around him. Doré's work, like Daumier's, combines both. This book, put together with a quite musical sense of rhythm, is full of unforgettable portraits and scenes—Doré, in a whirlwind, produced more than 500 woodcuts for it—and it will be an enthralling experience for readers interested in both history and art. (One can also detect here why Doré the cartoonist has been considered to be the "father of the comic strip.")

In his own life-time Doré became widely known for his illustrations to Dante's *Inferno* (1861), *Don Quixote* (1862), the Bible (1866) and *The Wandering Jew* (1866) and is generally recognized for his contribution in establishing the illustrated book of large format. Even in his best work, in his Rabelais and Münchausen albums, there is the romantic love of the grotesque; but his political interests and social emphases, so strong in this Russian work were also echoed later in his studies of London (only recently reprinted).

In a recent appreciation of Doré's work, the famous European critic, François Bondy, has called attention to the rhythmic impulse and the "musical variations," and has emphasized Doré's own musical education as a violinist and the influence of his brother Ernest who was a composer. In Bondy's phrase, Doré's *Histoire de la Sainte Russie* was "a score for the eye," with subtle and calculated changes of tone and tempo. "Indeed, this combination of a musical principal with a cabarettistic element make of Doré's achievement something more than simply caricature. The captions and the graphics hang together, not unlike the collaboration in Offenbach's operettas, only here Doré is his own librettist. . . ."

The words themselves, as Professor Richard Pipes (of Harvard University) emphasized in the new introduction to this edition, have an importance and special interest. Beyond the puns and the obvious political tendentiousness (an anti-Russianism which Doré shared with most of his contemporaries, including Karl Marx), there is an imaginative range and power. François Bondy has pointed out that a German edition was published in the year 1917, but the omission of some twenty-three drawings distorted the character of the work. Professor Pipes sets Doré authoritatively in the whole context of the image-makers of the Russian character, from the Marquis de Custine to George F. Kennan.

This new facsimile edition of Doré's *History of Holy Russia* (for which Daniel Weissbort has done the first translation into English) is more than an intriguing and amusing curiosity, it is a work of permanent fascination.

HISTORY
OF HOLY RUSSIA

Photo: Bettmann Archive

THE RARE AND EXTRAORDINARY HISTORY OF HOLY RUSSIA

with over 500 illustrations by

GUSTAVE DORÉ

TRANSLATED BY DANIEL WEISSBORT

INTRODUCTION BY RICHARD PIPES

THE LIBRARY PRESS
New York
1971

Copyright © 1971 by The Library Press

Published in English for the first time from
the original French edition (Paris, 1854):
HISTOIRE
Pittoresque, dramatique et caricaturale
de la
Sainte Russie
d'après les chroniqueurs et historiens
Nestor, Nikan, Sylvestre, Karamsin, Ségur, etc.
commentée et illustrée de 500 magnifiques gravures
par
Gustave Doré
Gravée sur bois par toute la Nouvelle Ecole
sous la direction générale de
Sotain
Graveur de l'Histoire de Russie, de batailles,
de portraits, de paysages, de genre, de fleurs, d'animaux,
de crustacés et de plantes rares.

LIBRARY OF CONGRESS CATALOG CARD NUMBER:
75-161410

INTERNATIONAL STANDARD BOOK NUMBER:
0-912050-11-X

PRINTED IN THE UNITED STATES OF AMERICA

INTRODUCTION

EUROPE "DISCOVERED" RUSSIA in the late fifteenth century in exactly the same sense that it discovered the Indies — a *terra incognita* peopled by an alien race — and ever since its attitude toward that semi-European, semi-exotic country has vacillated between scorn and fear. On contact with uncompromisingly black or yellow heathens, the European could, with some effort, allow for a fundamental dissimilarity and adopt an attitude of tolerance. He might even find amusement in seeing himself through the eyes of an imaginary barbarian or a Persian sage. But what could he make of a white people who worshipped the Cross, and yet were so different in the way they thought or behaved? Unlike the Africans, they were not children; unlike the Persians or Chinese, they were not heirs to an ancient civilization. They were rather a kind of caricature of civilized men, just enough of both savage and urbane to make them amusing and (under some circumstances) menacing.

At first, they seemed mostly amusing. As early as the seventeenth century Swedes called them "bears", and the nickname spread. There were endless jokes about the legendary cold of Russia: it was said that in the depth of the Russian winter words transformed themselves into letter-shaped icicles the instant they left the speaker's lips, so that one read rather than heard what people said. The commanding figure of Peter the Great for a while gained Russia respect. But his female successors, those sybaritic tsarinas with their endless lovers, barbarously mingling ostentation with cruelty — what inexhaustible subject for the wits of the eighteenth century! About Catherine the Great there were hundreds of anecdotes, most of them apocryphal, but this fact did not prevent them from acquiring a life of their own and passing intact from generation to generation. Not a year passes that some undergraduate does not ask whether Catherine really met her death in the embraces of a stallion. (The truth is, of course, that it was the beast that collapsed from the exertion.) A. V. Bilbasov, Catherine's biographer, compiled a work of two volumes which merely lists the titles of Western-language books devoted to Catherine. A good part of them is contemporary and scurrilous.

Then came Russia's revenge: 1812. It was Alexander I, the "Kalmuck prince", as Castlereagh was to call him, at the head of an army of allegedly illiterate and decadent landlords and barbarian muzhiks, who broke the finest army Europe has ever put in the field and freed the continent from Napoleon's domination. It was no use for Napoleon to spread the legend he had been defeated by the Russian winter (see p. 133 of this book): in reality, by the time severe winter had set in his Grand Army was well along on its grand retreat, a sadly decimated mob. Nor could the victory at Waterloo obscure Russia's achievement: for no matter what its outcome, in 1815 nothing could have restored Napoleon's lost empire. Europe knew all this deep in its heart. Hence its dread. For suddenly on its periphery appeared an overwhelming and uncontrollable power whose very existence upset the delicate international equilibrium of which it was proud and on which its prosperity depended.

The obverse of fear is rage. In the forty years which elapsed between Napoleon's disastrous campaign and the Crimean War, a swelling tide of Russophobia spread across Europe. Whatever the issues dividing them, liberals and radicals were as one in their hostility to Russia. This was the time when the apocryphal "testament" of Peter the Great, plotting world conquest, circulated everywhere, and all believed Russia was covered with Potemkin villages. Nearly every modern myth and prejudice about Russia and the Russians came into being during this period.

And, indeed, there was something to fear. Nicholas I (1825-1855), a martinet to the marrow of his bones and a born conservative, swallowed Metternich's theories intact, without diluting them in that cynicism and worldliness with which they were meant to be taken. Employing traditional Russian means — bureaucratism and lawlessness — he earnestly sought to transform Russia into a regimented "command", run like a Prussian barrack. He was so afraid of an imminent collapse of civilization from the twin onslaught of liberalism and free thought that he placed the resources of his country at the disposal of any where social stability and political legitimacy seemed threatened. In this spirit he offered to crush the February Revolution in

France and in 1849 actually sent troops into Austrian Hungary. His inexorable pressures on the Ottoman Empire, his thirty years' war against the mountain people of the Caucasus, his merciless repression of the Polish uprising of 1830-31 — all furnished evidence that he was in earnest. And considering that he disposed of the largest standing army in the world (his cavalry was reputed to exceed of all that the European powers combined) the alarm he inspired was natural.

During Nicholas's reign, Europe was flooded with books intended to capitalize on the new interest in Russia. They ranged from slender vignettes of one social season in St. Petersburg to earnest treatises, like the triple-decker published by the agrarian expert, August von Haxthausen, who had traversed the empire, notebook in hand. The most sensational of these works appeared in Paris in 1843 under the innocuous title *La Russie en 1839*. Its author, the Marquis de Custine, came from an old and distinguished French family. Having become ostracised from Parisian society because of involvement in an allegedly homosexual incident, he turned his attention to literature. In 1831 he published an account of his travels in Spain. The book enjoyed only moderate success, but Balzac was greatly impressed by it and urged Custine to write more travel books. Balzac's encouragement, coupled with the immense popularity of de Tocqueville's *Democracy in America* (1835ff) and close connections with Polish emigres, persuaded Custine to undertake a literary journey to Russia.

He spent in Russia only three months, but he gathered enough impressions to produce in one year a four-volume work. (How did nineteenth-century authors write at such a pace? Balzac gave the answer: one page a day gives one book a year, two pages, two books, and so on.) *La Russie en 1839* enjoyed immediate success: it is reputed to have sold 200,000 copies. As an historic source, the book ranks low, and does not even have a place among the "accounts of foreigners" listed in manuals of historiography. Its value lies elsewhere. By some intuition, possibly rooted in homosexuality, de Custine was aware of that which other travellers had missed: the atmosphere of the country. He noted the undercurrent of violence and pessimism beneath the glacial order of Nicholaevan Russia; the expansionist implications of the Russian desire to be something other than they really were; the spirit of Muscovy lurking behind the rococo facade of St. Petersburg. Haxthausen's learned treatise in incomparably more valuable to the historian of nineteenth-century Russia; but de Custine's impressionistic account tells us astonishing things about the Russia of the future. Mr. George Kennan, who, like several other diplomats, was amazed by the relevance of *Russie en 1839* while serving in the Soviet Union writes: "Even if we admit that *La Russie en 1839* was not a very good book about Russia in 1839, we are confronted with the disturbing fact that it was an excellent book, probably in fact the best of books, about the Russia of Joseph Stalin, and not a bad book about the Russia of Brezhnev and Kosygin."* The mystery of such intuition remains to be solved.

Gustave Doré was 22 in 1854 when the Crimean War broke out, an unknown cartoonist employed by Philippon's *Journal pour Rire*. The mood in France was revanchist and in this, his first independent publication, he made a direct appeal to it. De Custine's spirit hovers over this volume. We see de Custine on p. 141 trembling in his St. Petersburg bedroom while police spies, like rats, creep around peeking and sniffing. There is much more on these pages drawn from de Custine, including the well-known account (illustrated at the bottom of p. 145) of Custine's conversation with a Prussian innkeeper who observed that Russians always appeared gay when leaving Russia and depressed when returning to it. I am told that an abbreviated translation of de Custine published in the Soviet Union in 1930 (which I have not been able to consult) was illustrated with Doré's drawings.

George F. Kennan, The Marquis de Custine and his Russia in 1839 (Princeton, N.J., 1941), p. 124. I should like to note in passing a curious phenomenon: the ability of dilettanti gifted with insight to understand that which can elude the most learned experts. Sydney and Beatrice Webb, those paragons of English socialism, admirably cautious in their judgment, emerging from a mass of reading on the USSR, published in 1937 their Soviet Communism: A New Civilization *a book which can be charitably described as balderdash, and more accurately as an obscenity. At a time when millions of Russians were being tortured, exiled and shot on Stalin's orders, the Webbs concluded (note the pseudo-academic tone!) "It would, we think, be difficult for any candid student to maintain that the USSR is, at any point, governed by the will of a single person — that is to say, a dictator" (Vol. I, 2nd ed., p. 429). Six years earlier, even before the character of the regime had disclosed itself in full, diminutive, wispy e.e. cummings took one look at the Soviet Union and in his* eimi *(London, 1933, p. i) declared it to be a Hell "where men are shadows & women are nonmen."*

If the content of this volume derives from de Custine, the manner of presentation is purely Rabelaisian. What in de Custine appeared subtle and somber, here comes out broad and absurd. Like Rabelais, Doré achieves the effect of ridicule by telling nonsense in a seemingly straightforward, deadpan, almost pedantic manner. The discussion concerning the relative virtues of the two-knotted and three-knotted knout (pp. 81-83) — carried on in Latin! — is indeed Rabelaisian. So are the repetitive pictures of barbarities. When foreign hordes invade Russia, its soil vanishes from sight, so vast is the multitude (p. 51); when Ivan the Terrible perpetrates his massacres, people literally swim in blood (p. 87). There are passages (*e.g.* the description of the birth of Peter the Great on p. 99) where the text is taken word for word from Rabelais, with only the names changed. Everything revolting or stupid is enlarged to Gargantuan dimensions. The natural affinity of Doré with Rabelais must have struck contemporaries as well, for immediately after the appearance of the *Histoire* he was commissioned to illustrate *Gargantua et Pantagruel*. It was this work which brought him international fame and launched him on his career as Europe's most successful illustrator.

Looking at these savage anti-Russian cartoons one cannot forget that in less than two decades the French themselves would be the object of nationalist ridicule. In 1871, as Paris starved under Prussian siege, Doré's German contemporary, Wilhelm Busch, brought out a series of cartoons in which — with much less wit but no less scorn — he portrayed the nation of gourmets forced to eat dogs and cats. Fun of this kind cost Europe dearly in the long run.

But there is another aspect to this book, reflected in its publication history. The Nazis prohibited from circulating in Germany an edition brought out just before they had seized power. Then, as the Soviet troops were about to enter their territory, the defeated Germans destroyed the stocks of the books for fear of infuriating their occupants. It seems curious that a book satirising tsarist Russia should displease the Nazis and be thought to displease the Communists. The reason, I believe, must be sought in the fact that Doré ridicules not only, and perhaps not even mainly, Russia, but also despotism. How very contemporary is the cartoon on p. 139, where actors sit comfortably on the stage, watching the spectacle of public adulation of the emperor! To those who in the name of the people (rather than of Divine will) demand similar adulation in our time, such cartoons must appear in bad taste; and hence we can be quite certain that this volume of cartoons will not appear in any country where the spectrum of political debate is still limited to the chore between a two-knotted and a three-knotted knout.

RICHARD PIPES
July 1971

Richard Pipes is Professor of History at Harvard University and Director of its Russian Research Center. Among his books are a study of Russian nationalism (1964) and a biography of the Russian liberal Peter Struve.

HISTORY OF HOLY RUSSIA

O rus, quando te aspiciam!
—Horace

Qui les meut? qui les poinct? qui les ha ainsi conseille? Ho, ho, ho. ho! Mon Dieu, mon saulveur, aide-moi, inspire-moi, conseille-moi   —Rabelais

—Confucius

The origins of Russian history are lost in the mists of antiquity.

It is only towards the IVth century that this history begins to take shape.

But its first period has nothing of interest to offer.

A HISTORY OF HOLY RUSSIA

The earliest chroniclers tell how round about the year 2 or 2½, the handsome bear Polnor was enticed by the lazy smile of a young walrus and that from this sinful union sprang the first Russian. (Nest.: ap.: et ecc.; gloss. Conrad.; apud. Sev.!:? et q.s.)

According to others, however, it was a *penguin* not a walrus. (§ 11C, eccl. t. 816: et apud Gall.: int.: et contra: § 11X11V etenim vero: ? sed in. imp.: de tit. 181.)

And indeed, learned men ever since have been cudgelling their brains, forming the most hair-raising theories on the subject.

But let us not be confused by this flood of useless learning.

I shall advise you, my dear reader, to assume the above skeptical and lofty expression in the face of what only mad erudition or blind hatred of all things Russian could have inspired.

Besides, to return to the origins of this tedious history would be like climbing the Urals or . . .

an icily cold undertaking.

A HISTORY OF HOLY RUSSIA

At last we come to that period where the historian, on the basis of important and authentic documents, may, if he be gifted and succinct enough, achieve a certain lucidity, coherence, even interest.

The Essklwons, or Esclavons, or Sclavons, later Klaws, Slavs or esclaves, from the word *slavia,* which in their tongue means glory, were identical with those Wepdrognwians or Wolpolodrgswlians or rather Pechenegs who have so often invaded the northern regions and whom we shall later encounter, under the name of Golwsphrians or Susplglpdswiths (the corrupt form of which is Poldniwgkarikss), crossing the Dwlarzwirrwka (the Dnieper or Dnepr of today), where 56,813 of them, not counting old men, women and children, were drowned, and mingling with the Threrwpnmdplwiss or Prtwpdnckgnian races, commonly known as Voguls, Cheremis, Chuvash, Permians, formerly Biarmians, Finlanders, Lapps, Estonians, Rusalki, Polovtsy, Khazars, Kiwiwts, Whgptstv, Huns, Bulgars, Ugrians, Krwngpthgntkls (Hragnwkpstwsklmtss being erroneous), etc., etc., etc., etc. These wandering peoples led a pastoral life as *pastores, pastyri,* or *pastovkli.* They were known by these names as they grazed their flocks (*pascere, pastifera, wer,* which in Greek means possess. But to return to our subject. These shepherds counted their wealth in sheep, *oves, ovsti,* They had to protect themselves against wild animals, even under the Attics, and with the digamma (facio, facere, dormio)

A HISTORY OF HOLY RUSSIA 7

The next century being as tedious an affair as the last one, I would be frightened of setting my reader against this book from the start, wearying him with a plethora of dull sketches. However, my publisher, being a conscientious man, has insisted that I leave spaces at this point to show how an astute historian may render all things palatable while excluding nothing.

A HISTORY OF HOLY RUSSIA

Sacrifice to Perun of citizens accused and convicted of freedom of speech.

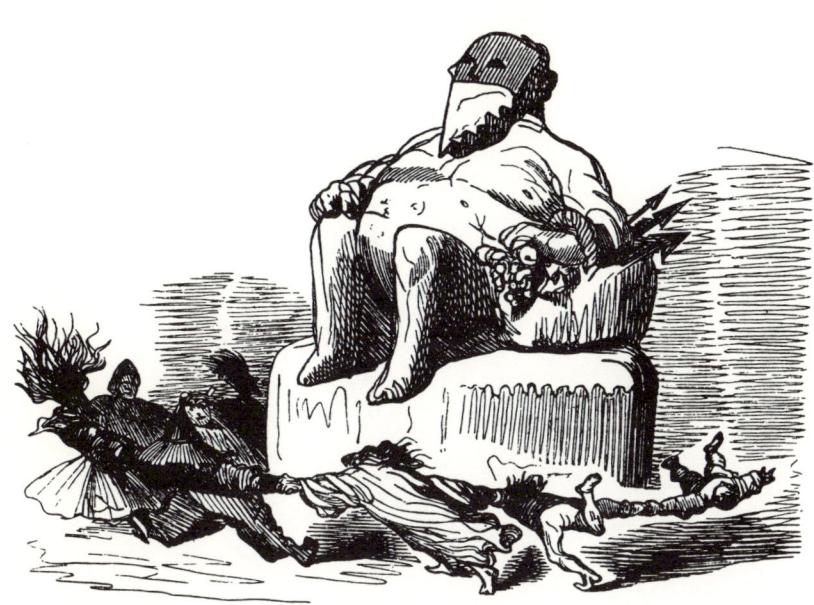

The ancient Russians worshipped Perun, god of peace, harvests, armies, friendship, commerce, war, honor, glory, guile, lying and orthodoxy, etc., etc., etc.,

This religion expressly required that snakes and other reptiles be worshipped.

The priests lost no opportunity to enforce this rule by means of the whip. It is also from this remote period that the knout dates, the word "knout" signifying, in the concise and expressive Slavic tongue, a most reliable and forceful method of persuasion, the only one, indeed, capable of persuading the ancient Russian to abandon his savage ways.

The ancient Russians had a high regard for women, and tended to allow themselves to be led by them in everything.

A HISTORY OF HOLY RUSSIA

Weary of being governed by its instincts and desires, the Russian nation decides one day to appoint a leader.

With the dispute concluded, the parties agree on one point: that it requires a complete man to govern a nation. Efforts are made to discover such a man among the survivors, but no one whole enough to assume command is found.

They have, therefore, to call on their Asian neighbors to send them some men to choose from.

On emerging from the chest, Rurik makes good his claims by proving then and there that he has a sharper mind and, above all, a steadier head than his brothers.

A HISTORY OF HOLY RUSSIA

Scarcely has he ascended the throne than Rurik marches on Constantinople.

Then he returns

and dies of kidney pains.

Igor, his successor, marches on Constantinople,

and returns to Novgorod,

where he soon dies of kidney pains.

Oleg, his successor, marches on Constantinople,

and returns home

where the family complaint soon disposes of him.

Stricken by this same illness (*tsarina colica*) Isyaslav, on his accession, consults his doctor who hastens to assure him that he is imagining it all and that he need only take the waters of the Black Sea in the smiling land of Turkey.

Cheered by these words, Isyaslav travels there announcing that he will return home stronger than a Turk.

Isyaslav, on his way back, curses the unfavorable winds.

But the welcome he receives at this health resort so vexes him that, in a blind rage, he smashes all his ships.

But when even more unfavorable winds blow, he breathes his last breath.

A HISTORY OF HOLY RUSSIA

Vasily, a vigorous and quick-witted man, at once takes advantage of the general disarray to proclaim himself Isyaslav's successor and cries out at the top of his voice that there will be but one anchor, that being himself.

The unlawfulness of the succession has a profoundly loosening effect on public morality, and his son Igor, outraged at this, induces in his father certain alarming symptoms.

— But enough about colic. I do not know how much further my detachment, on the one hand, and sense of propriety, on the other, will allow me simply to describe events as they were.

Igor, his successor, hastens to Constantinople and informs the Porte's door-keeper, who is reluctant to release the catch, that he has come merely to propose a treaty — oh, but what a treaty, one that may be broken only at the risk of arousing the whole of Europe — and that behind him, moreover, are the men of 1812.

Whereupon, the Turks, who have never liked playing with words, show what they think of treaties.

A HISTORY OF HOLY RUSSIA

Upon Igor's death (1), the regent Olga acquaints the future Tsar at an early date with the exigencies of Russian politics.

She also shows him how total solitude can develop the intellect concentrating the mind on Socrates' celebrated dictum, so appropriate for tsars, (know only thyself).

However, the wise Olga does not neglect the young Tsar's physical education either, submitting him to rigorous military discipline.

The wise Olga is more than a match for the various exalted parties courting her, extinguishing her suitors' ardor with all speed.

Immediately after, the thought of this outrage against public morality brings a blush to her cheeks.
Oh what has become of the fierce virtues of former times!

When, that same day, at supper, her ministers inform her that the country is suffering from internal disorders, this stern—but just—princess makes them eat their words.

With peace reigning throughout the land, the wise Olga turns her gaze eastwards.

(1) *It is by now unnecessary to describe the manner of a tsar's passing.*

A HISTORY OF HOLY RUSSIA

Learning from the experience of her predecessors, all of whom had failed to make an impression on Constantinople, Olga, with female cunning, hits upon the idea of setting fire to the town by means of sparrows bearing lighted fuses.

This device, however, proves ineffectual.

Then, deploying her principal natural attribute, her beauty, Olga assures the Porte's door-keeper that her passion for him could embrace the entire Turkish empire, but the fellow, whom polygamy has made more than a trifle sceptical, sees at once that the key she seeks is not the one to his heart.

I have too high a regard for Olga's beauty to tell you in what manner she met her death, but it is widely known that this queen whose heart was cold as ice felt it burning as her end approached.

However, the wise Olga had had sufficient foresight to crown her son before the nation.

A HISTORY OF HOLY RUSSIA

On succeeding to the throne, Isyaslav II raises an army and informs his neighbors that it is peace he seeks and that he is determined to procure it at any price.

His neighbors are unable to hide their surprise.

This is the final straw and there is nothing for it but to fight it out to the end. The first impact is, as may be imagined, tremendous.

Never in man's memory has there been so bloody a conflict.

The rigors of the climate furthermore render all attempts at strategy futile,

and cast so much doubt on the outcome of the battle that each side feels justified in claiming victory for itself.

The chronicler Nestor inclines to the view that both sides have, in fact, won.

While Nikon inclines to the view that both sides have been beaten.

Before leaving the field of battle, Isyaslav's son, a most humorous man, points out to his father that should the latter wish to continue ruling it would be in a highly dismembered state.

A HISTORY OF HOLY RUSSIA

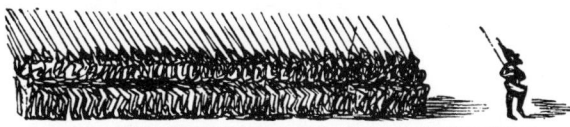

On his succession, Vyacheslav announces that he feels restless and must march on something, no matter what — his brother Mistlav for instance.

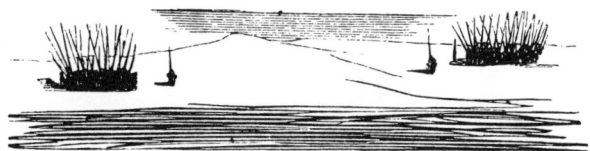

After several days of marching he comes upon the latter who has taken to the field with the same object in mind.

"Well, villain," he calls as soon as he catches sight of him from afar, "do you dare challenge me, pigmy, insect, louse, flea, bug, whom I would crush with a flick of my finger were we not kinsmen. Where is your might, where are your troops, where are your great deeds, miserable aggressor? You may well smirk — it suits you! But while there is still time, harken to my words, surrender your lands to me and we shall live in peace. Should, on the other hand, the treachery of your people or your own folly persuade you to oppose me, then your last hour has indeed come. Before taking such a step, observe the grim and revengeful figures arrayed behind me and remember that these are the men of 1812. I have spoken ..."

"Do I hear right?" answers Mistlav. 'Are my ears not mistaken? You speak to me of strength, to me whose empire stretches from the Don to the Tanais, whose very name resounds through the whole world which I could, if I so desired, take — to me, the great Crocodile, the great leader ... Your boasting will cost you dear! Brother — I pity you! You have just condemned yourself to death; yes, you are doomed and you have brought it on yourself."

"Barbarian, all you needed was this gift of gab. You really make me laugh. Certain matters are too funny for, etc., etc., etc."

"Easy, my friend! So, you choose to jest. Even so, good brother that I am, I am glad that you should enjoy these last moments, as, etc., etc., etc."

A HISTORY OF HOLY RUSSIA

"Come now! On guard, scoundrel, are we here to banter words ... You are doomed, but try at least to die as a man ... etc., etc., etc."

"And now, if you wish to proceed, so be it ... Just one word more though: my lands stretch from the Don to the Tanais; my empire, the only empire in the world, of which it occupies a third, my empire, I say, etc., etc., etc."

"You have gone too far, miserable braggart. You will learn what a tsar's wrath means! I shall not spare you or your men. Tonight I shall drink from your skull. And you, men of 1812, bestir yourselves, strike, charge, it is no longer a nation but a tsar you are defending!"

"Die then, if that be your wish; and since you are clearly out of your mind, I shall see that it is scattered far afield. But, as, etc., etc., etc."

"But why should I demean myself bandying words with you? Do not think either that I would humiliate myself by engaging you in hand to hand combat. Send me your champion, and I shall do the same."

"That is exactly what I was about to say to you."
NOTE. There is no room here for the full text of these verbal exchanges, which may, in any case, be found in Volume II of the *Chronicles* of Nestor.

A HISTORY OF HOLY RUSSIA

Into the arena Vyacheslav then sends a Bulwark of the North, otherwise called "the mighty Savoyard," a man of forbidding appearance.

But Mistlav is unabashed and produces the most broad-shouldered athlete in his empire.

The outcome of this curious match belies general expectations.

So the Varyagi at once announce that they have been taken by surprise and that, therefore, the fight must be declared null and void and be fought again. The Russians who regard the charge as totally unfounded, immediately reject this imputation. However, everyone knows the value of such protestations. The argument, therefore, soon transcends the bounds of ordinary political exchanges. A bloody battle ensues. The indiscipline, the many parties involved, the increasing number of Vyacheslav's enemies turn the issue into a real Gordian knot. Four usurpers – Richeslav, Wintkcheslav, Enuteslav and Furioslav dethrone each other in rapid succession during the conflict. The tsarist line is annihilated and the country plunged into total anarchy! But, after two years of conflict, Yaroslav, a wise and good man, a Russian but honest, generous and peace-loving, wins over the populace by his mildness and is recognized as Tsar.

A HISTORY OF HOLY RUSSIA

We come at last to the first peaceful reign, the prosperous reign of Yaroslav the Wise, who first brought the candles of knowledge to this barbarous people.

He rejoices at his subjects' eagerness to absorb the light.

Indeed, their fondness for *greasy* things makes them fight over it.

The following year, he establishes his celebrated Code, fixing a price for each limb torn from its brother, whereupon the proletarian, anxious to make an honest and comfortable living for himself, constantly seeks a beating-up at the hands of the rich.

One's anger therefore depended on the state of one's purse and citizens invariably did a little accounting before coming to blows.

One of the parties retiring at the sight of his adversary's purse.

This system enables the boyars to make pin-money from their ill-temper.

Yaroslav, feeling his end approaching, urges his five sons to love and support each other.

However, this lengthy period of peace imposes a considerable mental strain on the Russians who are more accustomed to shedding their blood at regular intervals, so that these wretched people are forced to ask the medical profession to bleed them artificially.

But after the wise king's death, the claimants set about each other with such fury that all that remains of them is their five helmets.

A HISTORY OF HOLY RUSSIA

On his accession to the throne, Svyatopolk, the only scion of this blighted line, receives envoys from Poland who sue for peace.

Angered at such baseness, Svyatopolk orders them to be cast to the beasts.

The Poles, astounded by this behavior, retaliate against the Russian envoys whom they incarcerate in dark dungeons.

Surprised by this brutal treatment of his men, Svyatopolk has it proclaimed throughout the land that the slaughter will at last commence again.

His people whom he finds eating heartily and having their fun, think that he must be joking.

At this, the Tsar's face turns such a deep purple that it becomes evident to all that he needs a good bloodletting.

On arriving at the field of battle, Svyatopolk realizes that his subjects possess a more pointed sense of humor than he has given them credit for.

A HISTORY OF HOLY RUSSIA

Smarting from the blows of his own people, Svyatopolk seeks help from his brothers.

Delighted at this excuse to make war, the latter persuade their subjects that a change of air is required for health reasons.

Their adversaries, who have got wind of this, hasten to advise a water cure, and offer them the river Stugna to bathe in.

But Svyatopolk, who does not appreciate the ready wit and jocularity displayed emerges from the water in a black mood, determined to take his revenge for this vile insult.

Upon entering the throne room, however, he is met with an even more jocular sight, his son, who expresses his astonishment at finding his father looking so in the pink.

At this play on words, particularly out of place under the circumstances, the wretched father, sobbing bitterly, asks his son if he is being serious. "Of course, father," answers Vladimir, "Far be it from me to make light of such a murky matter." Whereupon Svyatopolk, whose grief knows no more bounds, sheds tears and creates havoc about him.

Soon, even the most unfeeling member of the court (the Swiss guard) finds the whole affair heart-rending.

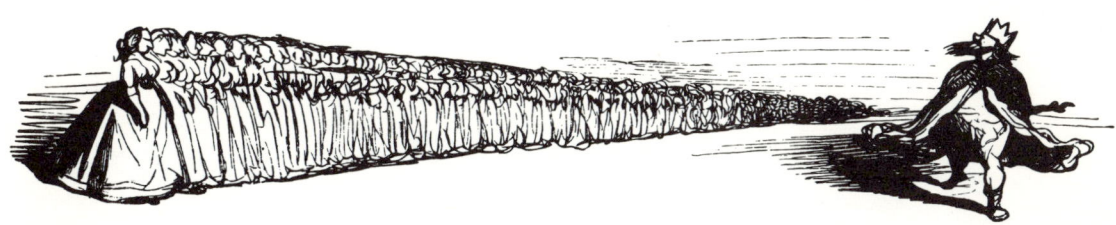

Bitterly lamenting a life so unjustly filled with sorrows, Vladimir suddenly remembers with sadness that the great of this world are not at liberty to give themselves up to tears. He remembers also the many exacting and cruel duties incumbent upon a monarch, the most important of these being marriage, that denial of the heart's dictates, that relinquishment of the freedom to love as one wills. Fearlessly, out of love for his people, he rises to the challenge. The fairest beauties of the land are accordingly assembled for him to make his choice.

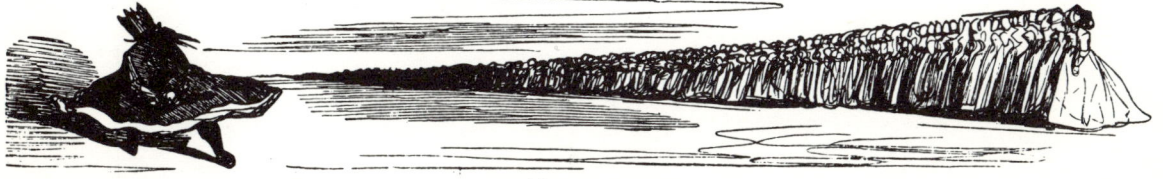

His affections waver.

To such an extent and for so long that, after three days of wavering, he finds that the women who have been brought before him are not so buxom as they appeared.

Even so, he does finally succeed in taking his pick.

Though true love has always seemed to Vladimir an essential ingredient of conjugal bliss, it is not without sorrow that he observes his spouses fighting savagely and passionately over him.

Indeed, so much depravity sickens him.

This sickness soon leads to his death. Feeling his end approaching, Vladimir casts a worried eye over his many offspring and for the first time ponders the evils of polygamy, in particular in so far as it affects a tsar. The idea comes to him to introduce at this late hour the right of primogeniture, but his strength is already ebbing away and what comes from his lips becomes more and more confused... he expires...

Upon Vladimir's death, his children agree that the succession is something to be fought over.

Russia is soon the arena of a vast civil war, each family becoming a separate party and defending its interests against all others.

After a year (heaven be praised!) the contending parties come together and agree upon the type of government that should be adopted. However, the merits and demerits of the various candidates to the throne still have to be discussed . . .

"If Vasily has strength and beauty in his favor," say some, "he will never possess the wisdom and vigor of his brother Mikhail. And let us not forget Gleb who is so gentle and eloquent." "What is all that," say others, "beside Rostislav's cunning." "The choice is obvious," say some newcomers to the discussion. "Roman unites all these qualities in himself: strength, energy, kindness, skill in battle, forebearance, etc." "Fie!" retort others, "Georgy outshines all these feeble rivals . . . etc., etc., etc., etc., etc."

"And yet," say the majority of these logicians, "why this stubborn and violent hatred, these blind consuming passions, these irreconcilable rivalries, these continual disputes? Is not this, infact, the behavior of barbarians?"

"Indeed it is," comes the response. "It is shameful for civilized nations to delight in the horrors of civil war."

"*So vile* a war?" reply the former. "How dare they speak to us in this manner. Thrash the insolent scoundrels . . ." Whereupon there is a further exchange of blows.

A HISTORY OF HOLY RUSSIA

Finally it is agreed that: "The egotism and ambition driving each individual to seek the throne can surely be controlled. Before coveting the throne, consider the responsibilities it entails. Besides, if everyone wants to be king, there will be no more subjects. Forsooth!"

It was in this unsettled period that the good chronicler Nestor lived. A monk of Kiev, he was the only man of his time who could write, and it is to him that we owe the foregoing account, which my respect for the chronicles prevents my altering in any detail. Alone in his cell, he did not realize that the monastery in which he lived was being demolished.

When the pillar supporting his cell was struck a violent blow, ink spilt over Nestor's pages, which explains the obscurity into which this period of Russian history is plunged.

The first legible line after the ink blot states that twenty years of conflict have passed, that the belligerents, at the end of their tether, have suspended hostilities, and that ties have been renewed.

That moreover Andrey has succeeded to the throne and that flat calm reigns throughout the land.

A HISTORY OF HOLY RUSSIA

Andrey is succeeded by Bruteslav, the great hunter.

Bruteslav is succeeded by Gobbleslav, the great eater.

Gobbleslav is succeeded by Banterslav, the great talker.

Banterslav is succeeded by Archerslav, the great shooter.

Archerslav is succeeded by Boundoslav, the great leaper.

Boundoslav is succeeded by Brawslav, the handsome one.

Brawslav is succeeded by Furioslav of the fine suit of armour.

Furioslav is succeeded by Drolloslav of the many plumes.

Drolloslav is succeeded by Beeverslav of the luxuriant beard.

Beeverslav is succeeded by Keeperslav, the friend to beasts.

Keeperslav is succeeded by Acuslav, the occulist.

Acuslav is succeeded by Cordiaslav the seducer

and later the lady-killer.

Cordiaslav is succeeded by Sporteslav the great horseman.

NOTE. I have not thought it necessary to state that each of these tsars in turn demanded the surrender of Constantinople and died of *tsarina colika*. But that goes without saying really, and to avoid tedious repetition, I shall assume that the reader takes these facts for granted.

A HISTORY OF HOLY RUSSIA

Sporteslav is succeeded by his son Scorcheslav who takes the opportunity of seizing the throne while his father is out prancing about on his mount.

But on his return, the father unseats the son.

Which does not please his lady wife who immediately makes him return what he has taken.

But the next morning, by 6 o'clock, the nation has already shown him that it is not to be abused in this manner.

Between 8:00 and 8:30, Yury, his successor, finds himself in a disputatious situation and immediately thereafter discovers how prickly a matter it is.

By 9:45, news of the secret negotiations leaks out.

But it should be noted that since 8:15, eight princes have succeeded each other on the throne.

Which gives the department of archives extreme cause for concern.

And the department of funerals too.

Towards 9:15 a bellicose party takes up the late prince's cause in Novgorod.

Clawslav who has been ruling for a quarter of an hour swiftly smokes out the germs of rebellion.

Seeing themselves compelled to burn for their beliefs, the Novgorodites lose their temper.

By half-past twelve, Yury's many supporters are already lamenting the passing of his line.

But the immediate and overriding need to establish a new principal of legitimacy upon which the throne may be based forces them to dry their tears.

A HISTORY OF HOLY RUSSIA

But let us return at once to the throne room where Crudeslav and his thirty-five offspring have already succeeded each other so rapidly that even the keenest of historians would have been unable to follow their progress. Each in turn, of course, has marched on Constantinople, criticized the Greek orthodox religion, died of vomiting, in short done everything expected of him.

The ease with which the throne can be siezed encourages a vast number of people to try their luck, and towards 2:30 they burst into the throne room.

Some of these succeed in their ambition, living and dying as true tsars.

But by 3:30, the crowd of aspirants in the palace has grown so large that there is no longer room to breathe.

On the stroke of 4:00, pressure makes the building burst.

The throne hurtles out landing in Moscow which henceforth becomes the seat of the empire.

And also the empire of sieges.

NOTES AND DOCUMENTARY REFERENCES

Greg. Nab. de hist. gr. et apud. valp, §347, tom. 8, in dissert. sub et adv. pro et contr. sed gen. et Cat. vol. 1;, §2341. Tom X111V1X. gr. R.S. pr. 1871. absc. controv. et diss. de super ind. A. B. oBr., S No 1, ind. in d. sed. pr. de histor. Slaw. et brev. glossarium et ling.?? (Tom. X11, SXV1, D. A. B. ( ). Atque Diff. Calpurn. S 6 ?? her. et Plin. Juv. de lat. et. grec. comm.? ling. T. X11. Grat. vuln. sed pro contra atque in vero enim. Crin P. X111, t. XV. Gr. hor. cord.? diem rebus.; cognose. 1893246, T. X11, Indiff.? (!) Br. et gr. gall. sin. seg. Mac et in   . Caln Bringzingocouz 169. voll. in octavo. Bris. Amsterdam 1349. – Et apud Sidn. od. magn. de nat. mosc. descr. et mor. brag. enim, sed? Atque G. V. X11 (.) de gloss. Valp. t. XV1VX1. De super contra. insc. non et in anno 1313. – 1412 vel in greg. anno 1411. – 1501 herod. regn. ins. gran. pro, sed, contra procul? Tit. V1, vol. de Insurr. Nord. et prec. inde; non (-) n X P N. 3191 gran. in. od. atque. prat. Tit. cat. sen. non inv. ( ) = :: anno 313, – 1417 premat. et philos. ant. et procul inde ven. 147. T. X111, S 12, spsr., etc., etc., etc.

These continual disturbances in Russia greatly dismay her Tartar and Mongol neighbors, who feel that the moment has finally come to take a hand in the affair. One should remember that up till now these barbarian peoples have remained tranquil and idle, and that idleness, with such people, is invariably associated with dreams of *occupation*.

The Russians, in their anxiety, hurriedly offer Uzbek-Khan, the leader of the horde, a vast quantity of rabbit skins in exchange for their ancient freedoms.

When this course fails, the Russians sally forth with spirit to the time-honored battle cry of *God and Novgorod are impregnable*, or else: 1812! 1812! return, return!

A HISTORY OF HOLY RUSSIA

Quite unimpressed by the resistance that is being offered them, the Tartar-Mongols inform their compatriots and the friends of their friends that it will take very little to conquer a country where men fight with battle-cries. Their friends do not have to be told twice, and a second invasion army is swiftly raised.

Others who have the patience to wait a few more days, are able to form a more regular army.

A HISTORY OF HOLY RUSSIA

And soon Russia is submerged under an ever rising tide of Asiatic barbarians.

The time comes when Russia is bursting at the seams and the barbarians, finding their movements somewhat restricted, conclude that they have come in too large numbers and that their eagerness has led them astray.

So, unable either to advance or retreat in the vicinity of the cities, they are compelled to bear the brunt of the fire rained upon them.

Once they have ascertained that the barbarians have been rendered powerless by the sheer weight of their own numbers, the Russians descend boldly from their ramparts and treat their enemies as one does cream that one wishes to turn into butter.

A HISTORY OF HOLY RUSSIA

There are so many dead and wounded Tartar-Mongols littering the ground that it becomes impossible to dispose of them, which soon leads to such deadly plague that the nobles are forced to employ extreme methods of disinfection.

Still under occupation, the Russian soil fails to bring forth anything, which leads to a cruel famine, a second calamity and one even more terrible than the first. The nobles endure it as best they can.

Meanwhile, Ivan, the shrewd heir to the Russian throne, taking note of his people's many grievances against their noble rulers, seeks to win the affections of the masses by cutting the ground from under the already unsteady feet of the feudal lords as they leave the table.

The next day Ivan, declaring himself Tsar of all the Russias, tries to gain popularity for himself by announcing that the principal blue-bloods should be bled first.

Then turning to his good people he asks them if they have been sufficiently avenged.

Sufficiently avenged, the Russians inform Ivan that they, in their turn, wish to avenge the Tsar by putting an end to the enemy incursions for ever. "But there are no more enemies," Ivan points out. "There must be some," answer his people, "and nothing in the world will prevent us from doing our patriotic duty."

A HISTORY OF HOLY RUSSIA

The Cossack volunteers soon come up with a horde of sorts, composed of men of good will and fair play.

But the latter gain the upper hand and kill 2,859,340 Cossacks, not counting old men, women, and children, and impose a war tribute of cattle upon them.

The cunning Cossacks respond readily to their demands, surrendering their finest beasts which, as can be seen, serves as a revenge for them, hence their name *Don* (from the French for "gift") Cossacks.

Despairing of ever being able to control his subjects' enthusiasm and convinced that they are doomed to failure, Ivan climbs to the top of the highest tower of the palace, from where he can follow their wild and unruly progress.

When he has lost sight of them he seeks consolation in the good Machiavelli's book, of which he had managed to procure a copy fifty years before it was written.

Which moves the unassuming autocrat to squeeze one tear from under his long, dark lashes.

Upon their triumphant return to Moscow, the Russian volunteers admiring their Tsar's lofty nature at once bestow the title of *Ivan-the-Great* upon him.

Accepting this glorious triumph in a modest and sober spirit, as befits a true son of Machiavelli, the wise Tsar teaches two of his commanders, who have grown excessively proud, to regard the victory rather than themselves as important.

A HISTORY OF HOLY RUSSIA

Emboldened by his success, Ivan makes a triumphant journey through the conquered lands, pushing even beyond the known frontiers.

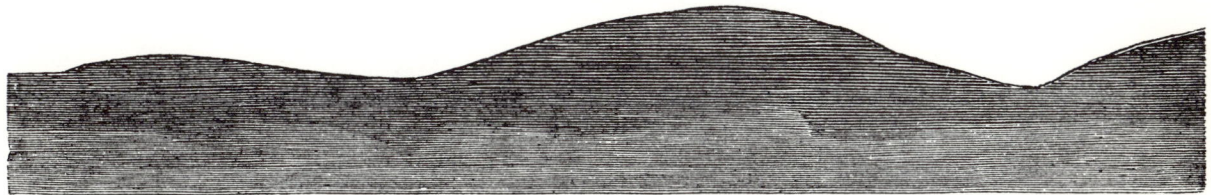

Crossing the mountains where the bear and the hungry she-wolf howl incessantly, he discovers the ice-bound land of Siberia, which seems to him a lawful prize.

So too it seems to his men, as he can see by the general astonishment of his frozen army.

However, the invaders meet with no resistance and a few simple badgers who have got wind of the recent invention of painting, misinterpret the motives for this invasion.

Ivan surrounds Tobolsk, the capital of this kingdom. However, he announces that he will immediately withdraw his troops if the King of Siberia has the good sense to allow him to take the few native badgers and sheep who subscribe to the Greek orthodox faith under his just and generous protection and if, furthermore (though this is of less importance) he permits him to rule the country just a little bit.

The Tobolskians are alarmed at this talk of *orthodoxy, good-will and fraternity,* and finding themselves outnumbered, surrender.

But the Russians, who are very suspicious and who have every reason to fear that their words are not being taken seriously, are determined to make sure that they are being told the truth.

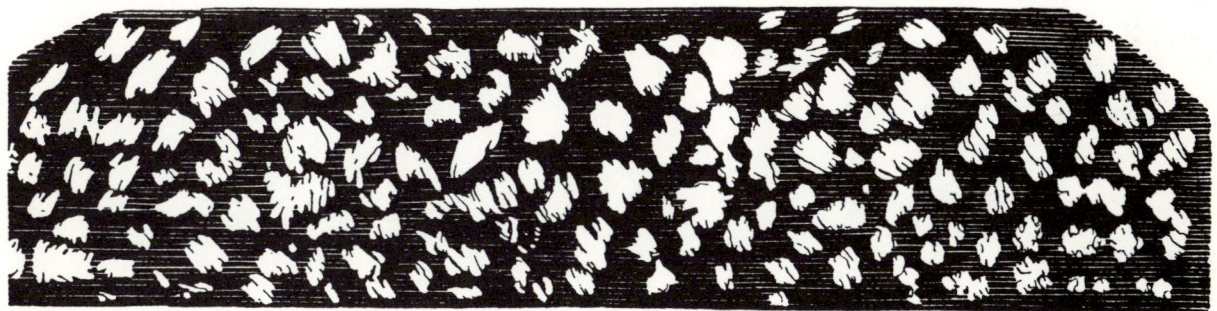

Meanwhile, it has started to snow, but in a truly Siberian fashion.

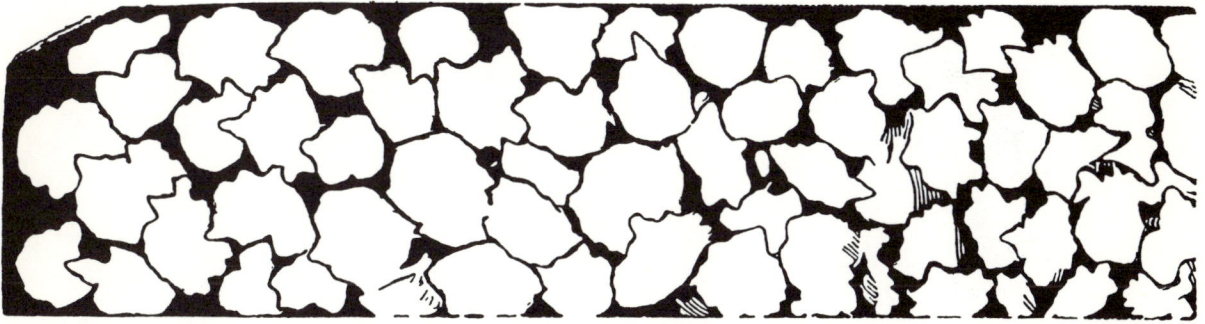

The sky grows darker and darker, the flakes larger and larger—no one has ever seen such weather.

When the snow has finished falling, the Russian army finds itself unable to move.

Whereupon the Tobolskians sally forth and, few as they are, disarm the iniquitous invaders without a blow being struck.

But the Russians, who in every situation always have a back way out, have managed to dig themselves tunnels under the snow that open into the empty huts, whence they hurl themselves upon their simple foes.

The Siberians, for their part, unwilling to let go of a single lance, advance armed to the teeth.

The Russians, by simply rapping them on the knuckles, show them how naive and foolish they have been.

2,750 Siberians, not counting old men, women and children, are at once put to the lance.

The rest are hacked to pieces.

A HISTORY OF HOLY RUSSIA

Only one Siberian is spared and used as a guide to the places of interest of this conquered land. The unfortunate native, finds it an unhappy turn of phrase when he is told that the Russians have had their curiosity prodded.

He first shows them examples of the animal and vegetable life of these hyperborean regions.

Then he points out a pack of nervous badgers who have been scared out of their wits by the sound of a leaf falling from a tree. "They're certainly a *harebrained* lot," says Ivan, smiling a royal smile. "But let's try to avoid such *brushes* as far as possible, as we don't feel like horseplay just at present."

Then he draws their attention to breakarmsandlegsinatrov, or in other words, the crevasses hidden under the snow. When the Russians find their attention too drawn, they ask their guide if he has not been affected by the jocular spirit of their Tsar.

A strong wind sweeping away the snow fortunately draws their attention away from this monotony and the Russians, who have not had time to catch their breath for two days, find that they are now being amply compensated.

A HISTORY OF HOLY RUSSIA

After which, the obedient guide shows them the sun, the moon and the stars. Deeply moved by his ingenuousness, the Russians point out kindly that these exist everywhere else.

Further on, he indicates the North Pole on top of a high mountain.

And then he shows them thirty-six candles.

However, as they approach the frozen seas, the weather deteriorates and a cold wind sweeps the hoar-frost into their faces which is most unpleasant and which, moreover, prevents them from taking their bearings.

When they reach the cetacean regions, Ivan asks his guide the name of the large creatures half-submerged in the water.

A HISTORY OF HOLY RUSSIA

They then have the opportunity of studying these cetacea at close hand and observing how they are caught. "Enough!" says the wise Tsar on his return. "Let those who would do likewise to me be sent here to fish these beasts."

Meanwhile, a chilly wind ruffles the face of the water, as also that of the Russians, who start worrying about how they are going to regain the shore.

When he sees the mines of this wild country, Ivan decides that it would be a good idea if those who would do likewise to him were sent to them.

A HISTORY OF HOLY RUSSIA

When he has finally had enough of all these wonders, Ivan orders the retreat to be sounded, but there is such a hard frost that the flourish of trumpets freezes in mid air.

Soon the horsemen, despite the speed at which they are galloping, start succumbing to the temperature and freeze to the spot. Reflecting on the matter, the wise Tsar now finds his ambitions for conquest cooling off considerably, but his good humor returns when he realizes how soon the settlers sent to this country will grow attached to its soil.

Then one of the soldiers gets the absurd idea of lighting a cigar, which makes him thaw out straight away. His companions are amazed that they did not think of this before.

But Ivan, who fully appreciates the ingenuity of the idea, makes haste to take the credit for it himself.

The thawing army reaches the frontier leaving a very clear trail behind it.

However, the wise Tsar, taking the view that his little guide has shown considerable levity, enrolls him in the light infantry and shows him the stick he's to get before he receives his marshal's baton.

Once back in his own country, Ivan is left in no doubt as to the temper of the employees of his meat concession, and is much taken aback by their hostility.

A HISTORY OF HOLY RUSSIA

Unfortunately, the changes wrought by war and by the rigors of the climate, in the appearance of the Russians make them unrecognizable to their savage employees.

But in their eagerness to set to work, the savage employees fail to notice that the transgressors are wearing pointed helmets: they realize immediately thereafter that it is they who have been given the going over.

There being no further obstacle in their path across the Urals, the Russians allow themselves to roll down the steep slopes, which is particularly effective as they quickly turn into snow balls.

On his return to Moscow, Ivan celebrates his conquests with great splendor, the main event being the execution in one day of the full quota of people due for execution over the year.

After which he sits down to dine.

However, before sitting down, he chases out a few tiresome individuals who have been holding court in the adjacent room.

Upon leaving the table, the wise Tsar pokes his nose out of the window and wonders what all the fuss and commotion in the streets of the capital is about . . .

At once he summons his priests (police-agents in Russia) who inform him sorrowfully that the Holy Orthodox Church is reeling under the blows of a terrible anti-Christ called Gutenberg who has arisen in Germany and has successfully imitated the multiplication of bread as it occurs in the gospels.

But the wise Tsar soon remedies this shameful situation by ordering an effigy of this enemy of God, Tsar and mankind to be burnt on the public square.

A HISTORY OF HOLY RUSSIA

In spite of these forthright measures, Ivan has to admit that the inventions of this heretic have had a profound effect on the Russian character. However, he forces his subjects to practise their progressive ideas in conditions of extreme secrecy.

But 'tis an ill autumnal wind that blows from the forests.

Anxious to rid his land of these vicious revolutionaries, the wise Tsar has a brainstorm, enlisting in his police force those individuals who can most easily infiltrate the secret Gutenbergian societies.

The despair into which he is plunged by the failure of these efforts gives rise to the most fantastic dreams.

His sleep increasingly disturbed, Ivan dreams that he has been called upon to repel new barbarian invasions. He cries out to his enemies: "If it is correction you seek, you have come to the right place!"

A HISTORY OF HOLY RUSSIA

The dream ends absurdly as do all dreams, and Ivan regains his calm.

But when he awakes, the sad truth of the situation becomes only too obvious.

There are so many that 100,000 men perish, not counting old men, women and children.

But scarcely has he restored peace throughout the land than the wise Tsar is saddened to see it once again subject to similar disturbances.

This time there are new outrages, new heresies. Mirrors, a recent invention, spread through Russia like a disease, and the wise Tsar, gaining access into a poor household in plebeian disguise, is horrified at the distress caused by this brutal exposure to reality.

In view of the effect that this invention is bound to have on serfs who wash their faces, Ivan makes haste to eliminate the danger.

His elder son reproaches him for this outburst, and points out that in politics breaking the ice (or mirrors) is a hazardous enterprise; Ivan, amazed at his wisdom, feels justified in handing over to him the reins of government in his new kingdom of Siberia.

A HISTORY OF HOLY RUSSIA

Ivan is also the first to boost Russian industry, concentrating initially on the blacksmith's trade, which he has studied personally. If, according to this enlightened prince, one wishes to cut a dash, one needs a sharp tool, and it is and it is not by killing only ten men at a blow that one can set about conquering the world.

Right from the outset, he distinguishes himself with the famous karkasmash and the celebrated blunderbuster.

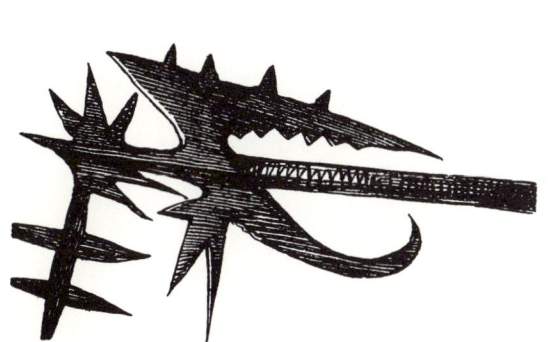

But this tireless reformer does not stop at that. These instruments are closely followed by the rumpsmasher.

Then by the buttocutter, which is a great boon to the law courts.

Then by the backed saw or file, an invention that throws much light on legal investigations.

1496!! The appearance of the disinvertebrator and the deobstructor, which set the seal on this reformer's glory.

But this is not the only sphere in which the wise Tsar displays his vast, encyclopedic genius. He takes up the abstract sciences, such as physics, chemistry, and pharmacy, and with as much success. It is to him that we owe the well-known *Treatise on Chemistry and its implications for politics*, (1497, Wagmann, Amsterdam) 3 vols. 8°; and Trswgndpqovkov, (Kiev, 1499), 3 vols. 12°.

A HISTORY OF HOLY RUSSIA

Proceeding from abstraction to abstraction, Ivan turns to the most metaphysical theories. He soon alters the entire philosophical outlook of his contemporaries. "Life," says this wise man, "is but a prison from which our faculties can liberate us."

People soon come to appreciate life at its true worth and to congratulate the dead on their happy deliverance.

As a further development of this theory, they begin to render each other the mutual service of deliverance from the hard bondage spoken of by Ivan.

"Let us," adds this wise man, "recognize only the sufferings of the spirit and, as true Christians, let us regard those of the flesh as an ordeal to which we are subjected by the supreme judge."

"Let us not forget, furthermore, that a well-tempered spirit is proof against steel."

"Indeed, what difference does more or less suffering make? Are we not our whole life suspended between joy and sorrow, hope and doubt, heaven and earth?"

And despite their hitherto barbarous condition, his wretched subjects cannot but admire their sovereign's penetration, and his trenchant manner.

A HISTORY OF HOLY RUSSIA

The knout, that wonderful invention upon which, as we shall see, Russian culture came to be based, existed only in a crude and imperfect form in Ivan's time. Even so, it did not escape the judicious Tsar's notice. He instantly saw its potentiality as a great civilizing force.

Determined, however, that the sublime and brilliant new line of reasoning upon which he has embarked should result in the establishment of something strong and stable, the wise Tsar decides to seek the advice of all the leading men of the realm and summons them to a solemn council.

Master Bludgeonov, who for years, at a great personal sacrifice, has devoted all his labors to studying and investigating this question in absolute solitude, opens the meeting with an exceptionally memorable defence of the two-knotted knout in whose merits he has long been a firm believer. "Gentlemen," he says, "the case that I am arguing before you is one that concerns the glory, the future of an entire nation. We are in fact, discussing the improvement and propagation of the knout among the poor serfs. There are two views on this subject: one inclines to the use of two knots on each thong, the other to that of three. I know that this is not merely a question of knots, but it is precisely these knots upon which our culture hinges and which secure the course of our advancement. For that reason I believe that no sacrifice is too great to ensure the wholesale application of this noble instrument. However, as the nation must of course be prepared to finance the benefits of civilization, the two-knotted knout, in my view, should be provisionally adopted in order that too great a strain should not be placed on the people's resources."

However, Master Shlagovitz, whose stand in all matters of orthodoxy whether religious or flagellatory, is highly intolerant, and who is renowned for his attention to detail, proceeds to attack his learned adversary.

"I have only one thing to say concerning my adversary's eloquent address. Russia has ever been guided by quotations from the Latin. You will tell me that this is really inexplicable in the case of a people whose religion is opposed to the Roman faith. But that is how it is and let us not meddle in matters that do not concern us.

"As true Muscovites, let us not stray from the true Latin path, as it is only by adhering to it that we shall conquer: *in hoc signo vincemus*. To my narrow-minded opponent I have this to say: he has failed to support his argument with any quotation. That is where he has gone wrong. I, for my part, shall sum up in five words: *Numero Deus impare gaudet,* or the three-knotted knout is pleasing to God. I therefore trust that you will adopt the use of a third knot. I intend, also, to answer my adversary later in the language of Virgil."

A HISTORY OF HOLY RUSSIA

Master Bludgeonov's Reply

"In view of my learned opponent's charge that I have made insufficient use of quotations, I admit that I may, indeed, have so far forgotten the solemnity of the present occasion as to have adopted a mode of address that is too plain and simple. I therefore hasten to remind him, in the words of the poet of Sulmona, that: *Perfusam merito natorum sanguine terram immaduisse,* etc., etc.,; *calidumque animasse cruorem, et ne nulla ferae stirpis monumenta,* etc., etc.,: and in the words of the poet of Mantua: *O fortunatos nimium si sua bona norint, Kosaqui,* etc., etc.: or again in the words of the Holy Scriptures: *Manus habent et non palpabunt, aures et non audient, pedes habent et non ambulabunt,* etc., etc., and many other things even more profound although they may not be Latin. I was saying that two knots is sufficient: *Quantum satis.* And also, *et deinde,* that if you pay, *aurum ducitis,* for the introduction of this civilizing instrument, *pacis simulacra praeferentes,* you ought at least, *etiam debuissetis,* reduce, *o felix quondam pecus,* the costs, *scires a sanguine natam.* Remember my lords, *nonne obliviscamini,* that for all to be able to afford this knout, *omnium quantorum, et quos ego . . .* it must be made easily and cheaply available, *usum praebere omnibus nonlicet omnibus adire knoutum.* That is why it is important to have only two knots. But to return to our good writers, and to cast a cursory glance at art. 6112 of the Penal *corporis* Code, §42., etc., etc.   . What else shall I say: *Trojanas ut opes et lamentabile regnum eruerint Danai,* and so much else besides which it would be pedantic of me to quote at length. I have finished."

"A single word would suffice to crush our honorable opponent, fool that he is, or, at any rate, twenty-six pages of Latin more ancient than his.

"Besides, in making use of quotations from so profane a source as that of the *Metamorphoses,* he must realize that he is speaking to the *void.*(anag.)

"I beg your forgiveness, my Lords, it is wrong of me to jest on so serious an occasion, and I shall conclude forthwith with a maxim taken from Cicero: *Ars politica tota est in knoutibus.* How can you deny *quosque tandem* the amount, *quot immensum,* of good done our subjects' skins. You forget that the Muscovite born and bred cannot do without the knout. *Beati omnes qui sub knoutum vicuntur.* Everything depends on the knout. *Convergunt omnia ad illum,* etc., etc. *Sinite ad illum venire Kosakos. Knoutus nobiscum quis contra nos? Sanguine aquemanu crepitantia concutit,* etc., etc. *Tertia post illas successit,* etc. *Saevior ingeniis et ad horrida promptior arma, nec scelarata tamen . . .* etc. And elsewhere, *insidiaque et vis, et amor sceleratus habendi,* etc. *Jamque nocens ferrum,* etc., etc., etc. Having considered all these technical points, let us now consider the question as a whole."

So eloquently has each lawyer put his case that the assembly finds itself unable to pronounce in favor of one or the other. It is obliged to have recourse to a simpler method of deciding between the two instruments.

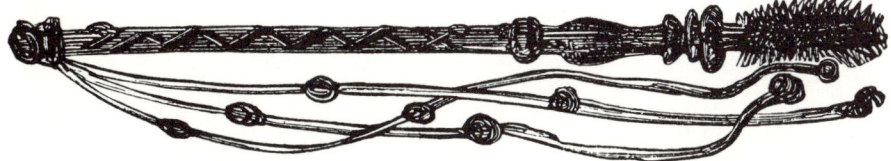

But when in practice it is found that they are both equally effective, it is decided to combine these two good ideas and introduce the five-knotted knout.

N.B. My dear reader, no doubt you think it heartless of me to have strained your attention with this dry and knotty legalistic problem. Perhaps you also think that I have invented or at least exaggerated the whole matter. It cannot be helped: when it comes to the knout, naught's impossible.

A HISTORY OF HOLY RUSSIA

By the end of this interminable debate, the members of the council are inclined to feel that Ivan, in his reformative zeal, is rather taking advantage of the diet. But the said Ivan, whose cunning intention it has always been to use Parliament for his own ends, sees his efforts crowned with success.

With this vital issue decided, the wise Tsar turns his attention to the cruel lot of women, which he has long deplored. He unyokes them and instead of this humiliating role, offers them everlasting peace and seclusion provided that they promise never to speak—even ill of each other.

It is clear that the great peace-maker has left no stone unturned to ensure the progress and advancement of his people! And it is to this end too that he introduces the practice of bringing engaged couples together for the first time at the foot of the altar.

Towards the end of his life, Ivan, as inventive as ever, in a last flash of brilliance, discovers the famous knockemov.

Such a plethora of culinary inventions inevitably excites the envy of the imperial corps of surgeons.

This venomous jealousy it causes the wise and excellent Tsar great distress, and he dies of his bitter sorrow.

The magnates offer the crown to the still young Ivan whom they find deeply engrossed in his studies and surrounded by his instructors.

A HISTORY OF HOLY RUSSIA

Some of Russia's subjects express their doubts as to the new Tsar's fitness to rule.

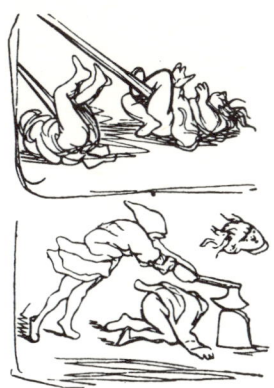

The following day they discover that they have been indiscreet and that his fitness cannot be doubted.

Seeing how swiftly the new Ivan dispatches these problems, his faint-hearted courtiers assure him hastily that he is certainly a prince who cuts a figure.

On his accession, the new Ivan decides that the excess of population in Russia is causing far too great a pressure on jobs and, to prevent any dangerous uprisings due to envy and frustrated ambition, he takes personal charge of the necessary reduction.

In the manner of the Germans who have just invented "dining to music," Ivan IV, also desirous of finding a means of mixing business with pleasure, initiates *"dinners with torture."*

When he learns of a rumor going around that these are the actions of a madman, Ivan the Terrible, who has inherited his ancestors' sense of humor, insists that on the contrary his heart positively bleeds for his people.

A HISTORY OF HOLY RUSSIA

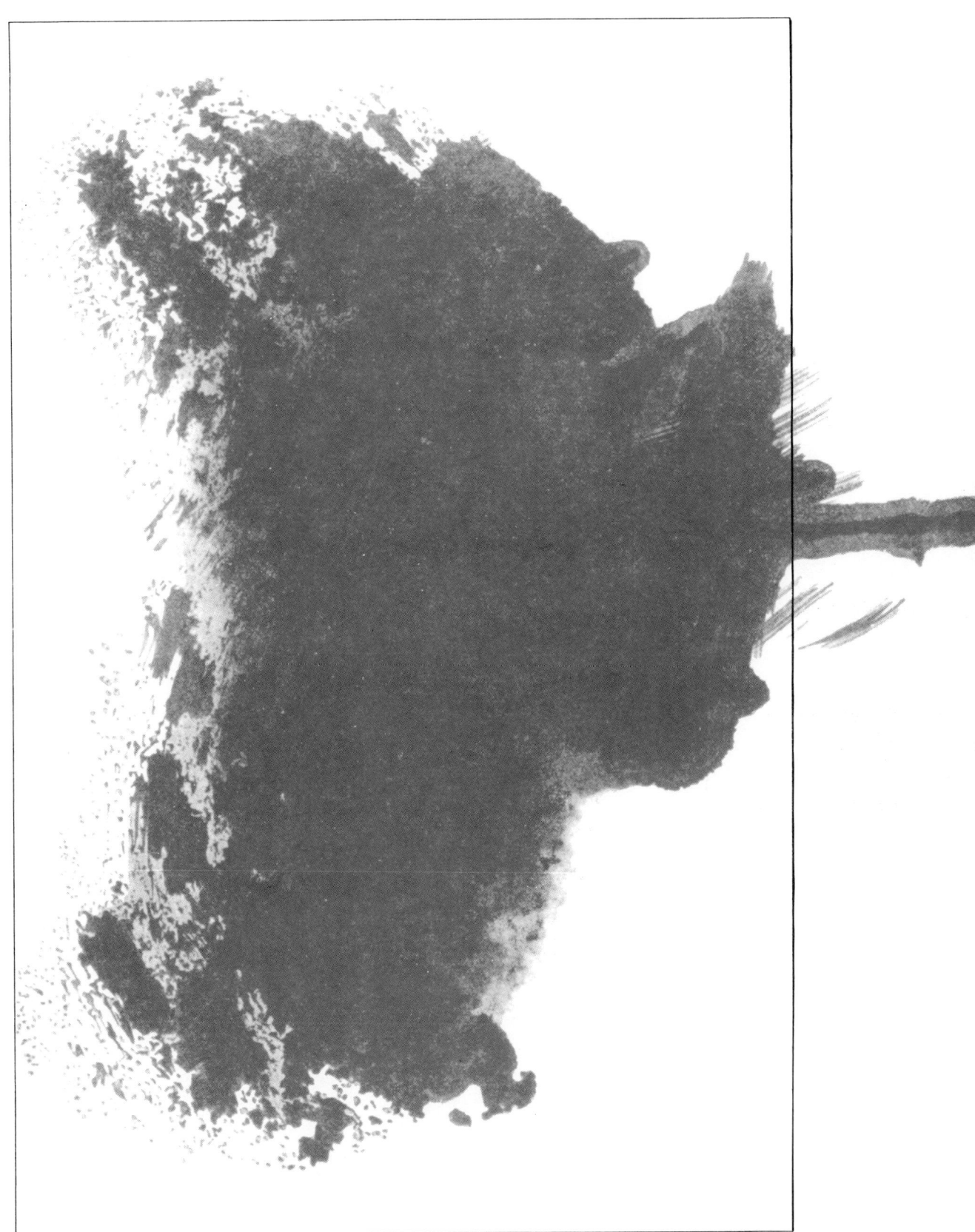

1542-1580. Ivan the Terrible's reign. Let us consider only the general aspect of this crime-filled period.

A HISTORY OF HOLY RUSSIA

However, by 1561, things become more presentable again. With advancing years, Ivan softens considerably and his methods become far less eccentric.

A HISTORY OF HOLY RUSSIA

By 1582, it is hardly more than a joke.

And by 1583, the terrible Tsar brightens up to such a considerable extent that he declares a national holiday, enlivened by magnificent displays and rounded off with an absolutely splendid piece of field practice.

The warmth and passion generated by this leads to the holiday being extended...

Taking advantage of the favorable conditions, Ivan follows the path of his predecessors and successors, asking the inhabitants of Constantinople if they are now ready to surrender.

But when upon his return home he is not given a sufficiently enthusiastic reception, he orders his rebellious subjects to be deported to Siberia.

After several months disporting himself in this invidious manner, Ivan is left with only two subjects and he orders them to deport each other.

They hesitate at first, but soon the autocrat's prestige and Russian submissiveness win the day.

His head turned by this frenzy of terrorism, Ivan the Terrible now really feels the crown's weight: a sad return to his early life.

A HISTORY OF HOLY RUSSIA

Sole ruler of a state without subjects, Ivan finds his solitude hard to bear.

His only consolation is the Orthodox Church into whose arms he throws himself eagerly, it being truly said that "When the Tsar grows old, he becomes a recluse."

This new life for the first time awakens charitable feelings in his breast.

In extreme old age, Ivan enters a second childhood and takes up games consistent with his former nature.

One day, while dismembering a grasshopper, he explodes with laughter. The manner of his death is particularly noteworthy in that Ivan is the first tsar not to succumb to the family complaint.

Some, not to say all, other historians have devoted more space to the reign of this monster, but, believe me my dear reader, it is as well to turn away from the spectacle of one who was as vile as he was worthless and tiresome.

A HISTORY OF HOLY RUSSIA

Ivan's great and noble heirs glory in cleansing the soil of Russia.

But they fall out amongst themselves and try to dispose of each other at a single sweep.

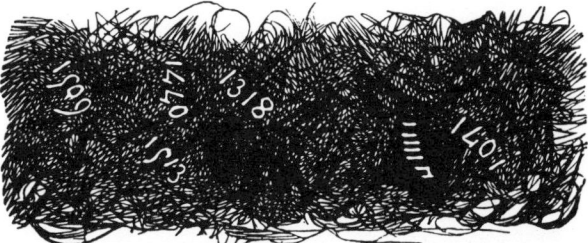

However, one thing leads to another; the factions spring to life again and frightful battles ensue. Each day brings new and more terrible conflicts. There follow massacres, catastrophes, excesses of all kind, and, for the historian, an even greater muddle than before. Out of this chaos, after many cruel years, emerges the Romanov dynasty, which inaugurates an era of peace and splendor for Russia.

And now, hats off to Holy Russia's mighty reformer.

A HISTORY OF HOLY RUSSIA

I shall leave it to Master Francis Rabelais, the first and only true historian of Russia and especially of Peter 1's reign, even though he lived 300 years earlier—well, nothing is beyond the powers of a genius with his inspired guesses and predictions!—I shall, therefore, as I say, leave it to this master historian to explain how this *very horrific and redoubtable* individual was born, what was his first cry, etc., etc.

"As soon as he was borne, he cried not as other babes use to do, miez, miez, miez, miez, but with a high, sturdy, and big voice shouted aloud, Some drink, some drink, some drink, as inviting all the world to drink with him; the noise hereof was so extreamly great, that it was heard in all the Countreys at once, from Russia to Poland ... The good man Alexis drinking and making merry with the rest, heard the horrible noise which his sonne had made as he entered into the light of this world, when he cried out, Some drink, some drink, some drink; whereupon he said, How great (and nimble) a throat thou hast, etc., etc., etc."

We meet Peter again as an adolescent in Zaandam. His natural predilections encourage him in the belief that he has been born to sap the foundations of things, and that in so great and arduous a task, actions speak louder than words.

He discovers charm and hidden depths in the shoemaker's trade too. Must a tsar, he tells himself, be duped one day by a shoemaker; and should he not ensure that the new society be established on firm foundations?

In this new craft, moreover, he discovers an effective way of shaping and softening his rough character.

Preferring, as can be seen, the study of practical skills to that of science, Peter follows this path with increasing confidence.

However, on perusing a book or two of philosophy, he finds the paradoxical side of it not unentertaining.

But his fencing and boxing instructor soon convinces him that this is not the surest way to people's hearts, nor the surest means of broadening one's point of view.

Believing, however, that he ought to dip into theology, Peter chances upon the proverb: *Vanity of vanities*, a sublimely true one, he feels, and applicable to those of his friends who presume to think themselves as great as he.

This restless activity results in his rapidly becoming ambidextrous.

But in so becoming, his eyes inevitably lose their gentleness, habitually looking East and West simultaneously.

Peter, whose noble purpose is to measure up to the challenge of his times, pushes generosity and self-sacrifice to extremes. He even acquires the vices of his own subjects, that he might better learn how to eliminate them.

A HISTORY OF HOLY RUSSIA

Judging himself now sufficiently accomplished to rule, Peter feels the moment has at last come for him to have done with his present pursuits and to mount the throne, which, however, he finds somewhat small for him, so great has he become in his mind's eye.

He makes no bones about putting down the many insurrections of the Streltsy.

Peter celebrates his accession to the throne in great style with an ukase unflinchingly annulling all previous reigns and Russia's entire past. His astounded subjects are of the opinion that the young prince is displaying positively superhuman energy.

On one occasion, at a court banquet, Peter, overhearing certain remarks that are passed over dessert, suspects that there are still a few unextinguished sparks of insurrection among the Streltsy. With considerable dexterity, he swiftly convinces those closest to him that ambition can make even the most sensible men lose their heads.

A HISTORY OF HOLY RUSSIA

As these after-dinner jokes become routine with him, it is impossible to tell whether, in receiving an invitation to dine at court, one has been invited simply for the pleasure of one's company or for one's brains.

Anxious to encourage democratic and liberal ideas in this country of slaves, and especially equality in the ranks, the great reformer sets an example, taking up the rear of his own army as a common soldier.

Later, he himself mounts guard at the entrance to his palace.

And ridicules his astonished generals.

In pursuit of his noble task of popularization, Tsar Peter seeks out his beloved Romodanovsky, whom he has jokingly installed on the throne, and commands him to refuse him his corporal's stripes.

Ready to risk his own life for his beliefs, Tsar Peter loses no opportunity of saving the lives of even the most humble and obscure of his subjects.

Mindful of the commercial needs of his people, Peter establishes an imperial fur bank on the shores of the Gulf of Finland.

Establishments of this kind greatly stimulate commerce.

A HISTORY OF HOLY RUSSIA

Charles XII defeats Peter at Narva

And is defeated by him at Pstvlqsstva.

Charles XII takes his revenge at Vlsqvtsva.

And is himself repaid in kind by Peter at Tsgvlstva.

But Charles recovers and thrashes him at Krvsqtpsva.

But Peter, undismayed, thrashes him at Grsvqtsvgptsva.

But Charles routs Peter's army in the vicinity of Skragvtsgrvtsva.

And Peter, in his turn, crushes Charles' army in the vicinity of Vstplgksqprtsvnsbtpva.

But at Pstngqlptrsntvqhstva, Charles falls in with Peter's batallions and cuts them to pieces.

But the latter recover and prouder than ever destroy Charles' north of Poltava.

Seeing that fate has reserved the last daisy petal for him, Peter no longer seeks to restrain his modesty. He walks the land with head bowed, and tells all comers how easily he might have been thrashed, he who had so foolhardily risked 2000 men against 200,000.

Eager to popularize the virtues of humility, Peter puts up posters bearing his modest thoughts on all doors throughout the land.

However, this modest deportment ends by making Peter stiff all over.

In his efforts to imbue his subjects with a proper appreciation of life, Peter exhibits the clothing worn by him at Poltava to show how life hangs by a thread. His subjects, who are less simple-minded than he thinks, see through this trick.

Peter accuses his saddle-maker of boasting that he lent him his punching-machine.

On the following campaign, Peter discovers that he has so successfully instilled humility into his people that they have lost all self-confidence.

A HISTORY OF HOLY RUSSIA

From the Collection of Russian Popular Prints *(facsimile)*

One day, while walking in the Moscow countryside, Peter met a plowman who seemed to him to be digging in an unintelligent manner, and leaping upon him he gave him a drubbing. "Plowman!" he said, "who do you imagine it is that has just thrashed you? Well, Well! I am your Tsar, Peter, called the Great, and to show you that I am not insensible to the tears of an obedient subject, I now appoint you door-keeper of the palace." This great prince was no less tender-hearted than he was quick to anger.

Another Popular Print *(facsimile)*

Tsar Peter, while walking one day in the Moscow countryside, met a plowman and addressed him in a most kindly manner: "What are you doing my friend, and why are you doing it?" "Sire," replied the poor man, "I must support a large family by the fruit of my own labor." Deeply moved by these words, the Tsar leapt upon him and crushed him in his imperial embrace. Not content with that, the great prince presented the widow with a pension and took all her sons into his army.

A HISTORY OF HOLY RUSSIA

For many years Peter has deplored the absurd and shameful superstitions of his still barbarous people and has dreamt of rooting out the evil that clouds their minds and obstructs their progress. However, before embarking on this difficult, dangerous, and colossal enterprise, he consults his star.

Nor does he forget to hold celebrations every Friday.

Peter's first action in this noble task is to put the law onto the tracks of a man accused of consulting spiders night and day.

Next he catches a farmer who is alarmed at seeing his salt-cellar overturned.

When, for obvious reasons, Peter has to admit that the enterprise is beyond any human being, he tries his hardest to forget about it.

The command is given to shell forests reputed to be bewitched and haunted by willis, gnomes, brisqlovsti or krvsqelptsnvi.

The purges continue.

On hearing this, King Louis XIV, as an act of courtesy to Peter, sends the latter certain artistic and scholastic articles which are received in Russia with great enthusiasm. Among these he has managed to slip a few laureates of the Ecole des Beaux-Arts and stylish painters; but this harmless joke goes unnoticed.

The following day the enterprising autocrat issues an ukase proclaiming that he has invented gunpowder.

There follows a second in which he declares that his subjects are incapable of inventing anything, and that Russia is open to all foreigners who are scholars or artists.

When some unruly subjects of Peter complain that a certain French performer, a fellow of little talent but much charm, has tried to persuade them that a bladder is a violin, Peter lends the latter his support against the misplaced patriotism of his own people.

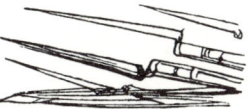

He lends the same support to the Beaux-Arts laureates who are finally acknowledged by the Russians.

This protection given to foreigners strongly encourages his own people to imitate them.

However, when certain of his Russian subjects finally impress him with their talent, Peter strongly urges them to be naturalized French.

At last Peter feels that the time has come for him to go to Paris. He embraces Richelieu's statue and exclaims: "O great man, I would have given half my empire to have learnt from you how to govern the other half."

This sudden access of Muscovite humility having failed to strike the hearts of the French with the intended response, his modest blush becomes suffused with a deeper red, and the next day he is back in Russia.

A HISTORY OF HOLY RUSSIA

Eager to build himself a capital more magnificent than all those that he has visited, Peter, who has been racking his brains over the choice of a site for a long while, chances upon a suitable one earlier than expected.

The engineers, who have to build the capital on piles and who are given only a fortnight in which to complete the work, realize at once that the land is highly unstable; it makes them apprehensive of what people (especially the French, who are a very tiresome nation) will say about the Petersburg court being founded on a bed of toads, reptiles and other slimy creatures.

The workers, for their part, are soon out of their depth.

But Peter, who is immovable where it concerns his country's honor, refuses to heed their faint-hearted complaints.

Examining the matter in some depth, the engineers try to persuade their Tsar to get to the bottom of things. Peter, however, finds the suggestion improper and shows his contempt by continually spitting out orders.

A HISTORY OF HOLY RUSSIA

In view, however, of the considerable popular resentment against his plans, Peter feels that the time has come to distribute largess.

Which stimulates his servants to a more fundamental study of the problem.

When the ground has hardened, Peter smiles the triumphant, dazzling smile of the genius who is finally understood.

Wishing to instruct his men and at the same time to set an example himself, he puts his hand to the task and begins by teaching them the art of pile-driving.

of shoring a wall,

of demolition,

of carting stones.

While marveling at the wonderful natural endowments of their sovereign, the obedient workmen doubt their capacity to follow his advice.

As soon as the plaster has dried, Peter wonders how to populate the new imperial capital as swiftly as possible and, powerful orator that he is, extols the melancholic location of the new capital by pointing out how well suited it is to the dreamy nature of the Slavs.

Encouraged by the magnificent achievement of having built a city on piles, Peter dreams of building a hanging city.

An underground city.

A movable city.

An under-water city.

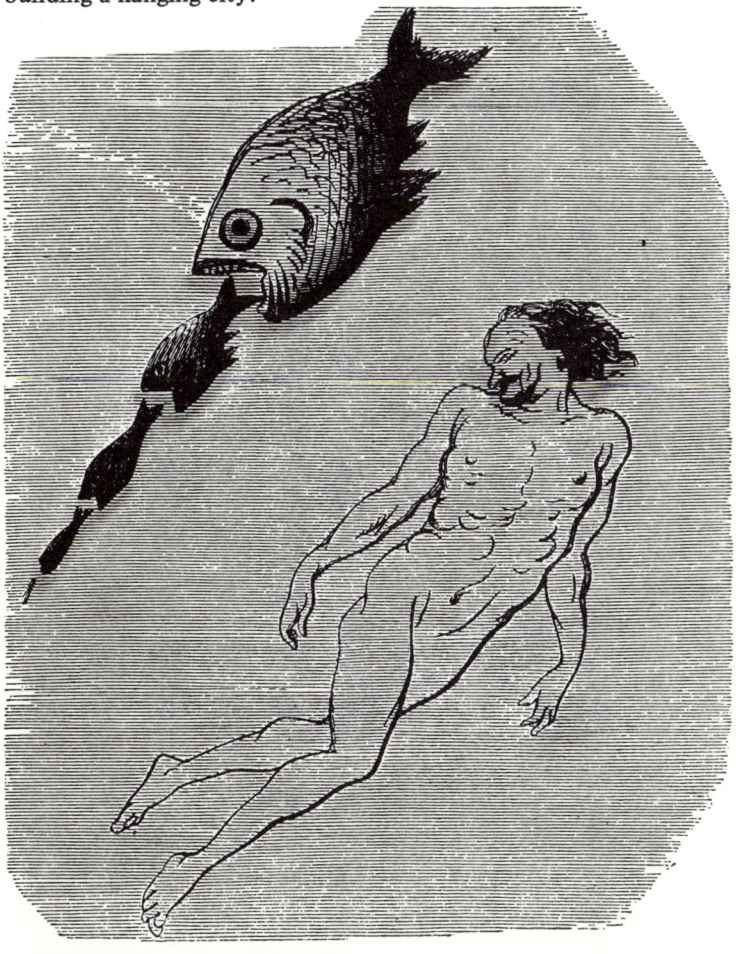

Gratified at finding himself in the same position as the astrologist in the fable, Peter, who is an excellent swimmer, takes the opportunity of having a bath and is amazed to witness the famous but hitherto unheeded proverb "Big fish eat little fish" being enacted in real life.

At this sudden illumination, Peter leaps from the water without dressing (Archimedes' system) and runs through the streets of St. Petersburg crying: "I've got it! I've got it!"

By evening, his mind is in such a dangerous state of turmoil that he tries to compose himself through gratification of the senses.

A HISTORY OF HOLY RUSSIA

The over-excitement and over-stimulation of this day gives Peter the most fantastic and ambitious dreams. He finds himself hiding behind the North Pole and unsticking the map of Europe from the globe.

After having unstuck it, he seasons it with tartar sauce and gobbles it up hungrily.

When he reaches the Western part, he discovers that the tartar sauce has glued England and France so firmly together that, try as he might, he cannot separate them. He is, moreover, unable to chew up what he already has in his mouth and finds himself choking.

In short, the jagged contours of France and England stick in his throat to such an extent that he is forced to spit out the lot after nearly choking to death.

Waking with a start, Peter reflects on this.

A HISTORY OF HOLY RUSSIA

But his appetite is so stimulated by the mere dream of swallowing Europe that Peter is unrecognizable on awakening.

He greatly alarms his wife Catherine, who begins to loathe him and to be unfaithful.

Ever since this unfortunate night, Peter's appetite becomes insatiable—fatally so. He leaves all his money and lands to his family, and concocts a witty testament, summoning some men of good will to his bedside to hear it.

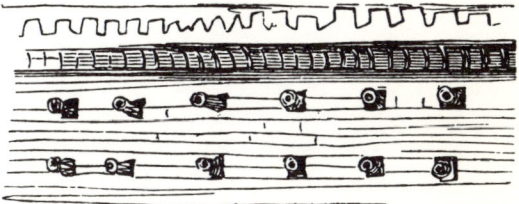

But soon after the great Tsar's death, his heirs discover that his estate is not easily appropriated.

"My friends," he says, sneezing three times, *"opus consummatum est* my hunger has undone me. I was too old to be able to satisfy it, but my noble aspirations I bequeath to you, who are young and vigorous. I go now to join my glorious ancestors, not Alexis, Michael, Ivan, Oleg, etc., but Alexander, Caesar, Attila, Pompey, etc., whose direct descendant I am. But before ascending to heaven, whence I shall keep a fatherly eye upon you, I would make known my last wishes, which you must swear to obey. Upon you falls the honor of carrying out the task that I should have begun had circumstances allowed me to. You must be aware that Europe is simply a province of Russia governed by ordinary men who bear the title of king only by my leave. You will remove them forthwith and you will annex these various countries to the Empire I am bequeathing you. If by chance—inconceivable as it may seem—these gentlemen resist Moscovization, then you must apply force against them as I have taught you to do. You, Knoutuzov, will succeed me and lead my subjects swiftly along the path of civilization: and remember, only the whip will achieve this aim . . . I am going . . . I am going . . . One more word, O Russians . . . Be merciful but relentless; be resolute and do not permit yourselves to be swayed by the false arguments of future ages directed against the noble spirit of conquest and insisting upon the inviolability of the rights of nations . . . Always carry your head high and scorn the present thinking only of the past, of Peter's prophetic voice that you are now hearing for the last time . . . Burn, kill, slaughter, if needs be, but do it nobly. Let Europe perish before Russia does. O Russians! remember the words of my ancestor: "Thou art Peter, and upon this rock shall I build my empire."

A HISTORY OF HOLY RUSSIA

The reign of Peter II.

The reign of Peter III.

Catherine II ascends the throne of all the Russias.

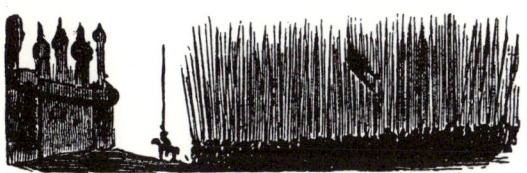

In consequence of this she arrives before the gates of Constantinople. A first summons to the city to surrender.

A second summons.

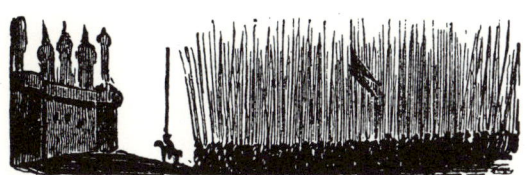

A third summons in the name of Orthodoxy, European balance of power, and the heroes of 1812.

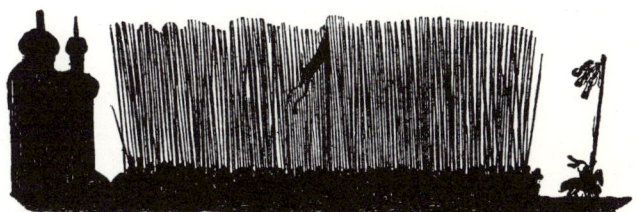

In view of the categorical refusal with which this is met, Catherine returns home without misgivings.

The Famous Treaty of Kuchuk-Kainardji

However, before returning to Russia, Catherine tries to reassure herself that the European balance of power will not be upset by these unfortunate events. She calls the Turkish leaders to Kainardji, where she signs the famous treaty in which she undertakes henceforth to have been completely deluded in believing that the time has come to seize Constantinople, and secures the Sultan's written assurance that the wars of conquest are to be postponed indefinitely.

Reassured on this point, Catherine returns to Petersburg where she gives herself up entirely to securing the affections of certain young officers. Oh, love, love. When you enslave us..!

A HISTORY OF HOLY RUSSIA

With European peace guaranteed by the Treaty of Kainardji, Catherine can, without mental reservations, give herself up to the pursuit of civilized pleasures and to surrounding herself with a court devoted to providing her with them.

You may be surprised, dear readers, to find a Roman rather than a Russian orgy depicted above, but have you ever witnessed a Russian orgy? If you have not, may God preserve you from it. If, like me, you have, then may God forgive you. You will, in that case, understand why I have not been able to represent it in a book intended for gentle folk. I have tried to dignify these indecent proceedings by setting them in Roman times, removing them, as it were, to the most remote period of history. It is, indeed, common knowledge that vice and debauchery in painting can only be acceptable on condition that they are in a classical setting, in other words, of good family. I myself am ignorant about these matters, but ask any painter of taste or a laureate of the Ecole des Beaux-Arts, and he will tell you.

Further on my pencil is outraged by Karamzin's account and refuses to serve me any longer. I beg it, I beseech it, explaining how I wish to make a name for myself; it hesitates.

There is nothing as full of airs and graces, as capricious, as my pencil when struggling with its bashfulness on the one hand, and desire for self-advancement on the other.

Finally, in a whisper, it outlines the next few pages of illustrations. The agitation that seizes my features and the blush that spreads over them are proof enough of my horror.

But that is not the end of the story. My publisher, who has contracted me to comment both with pen and pencil upon all the reigns in Russian history, has just reminded me of my commitments and accused me of disguising my reluctance to do the work under the pretext of being unable to. Not that M. Bry is a rogue. Far from it—he is a most proper publisher, his prudishness being almost proverbial. But, as a Frenchman and a Parisian, he is convinced that everything can and should be presented in a humorous fashion.

In the face of these accusations of disloyalty and threats of legal action, I am forced to submit. But how am I to manage it? Cursed be the day when I first set eyes on a publisher.

A HISTORY OF HOLY RUSSIA

My publisher's shameless insistence results in the matter swiftly being brought before the court of public morality. I exculpate myself with ease, first by laying the blame on Bry, then by proving that I had not yet read the historians when I signed the contract.

He has no excuse to offer and is humiliatingly forced to expurgate the pages of his book dealing with Catherine's reign, which ruins the edition and makes it less saleable.

A HISTORY OF HOLY RUSSIA

In the interest of historical truth, however, let us do justice to the few humanitarian qualities shown by Catherine.

Despite the many uprisings that occurred towards the end of her reign, she found time to establish hospitals, taking even greater care of wounded rebels than of other patients.

Under these hospitals several schools are set up, especially geological ones, where attendance is compulsory, but this sudden burst of activity tires Catherine and leads to her death.

Catherine's funeral procession.

The shrewd princess was determined to make her work compulsory reading!

Envying the King of Prussia's success with his memoirs, Catherine had intended writing her own, and the expression 'blue-stocking' dates, in fact, from the period when the Prussian blue faded on her page, she being the first woman to write. It is to be noted that this expression was particularly appropriate in her case because of the endless attempts at stylishness in her memoirs.

Catherine's rule and her deeds had gone right to the hearts of the Russians. This princess, generous to the point of expansiveness, had loved them so dearly she had spoilt them.

At this great queen's death, most of her subjects mourn her passing as no queen has ever been mourned before.

To her goes the credit for having eliminated all traces of the wild, rough character of the Russian, the old-style Russian, and for having softened his nature to the point where he may be taken at face value.

Certain noblemen, doubting the sincerity of this expression of grief, gallantly defend the late queen's honor. As a result, duels of every kind are soon being fought throughout the length and breadth of Russia.

A HISTORY OF HOLY RUSSIA

But, in view of the tremendous scandal occasioned by his mother's memory and the eagerness of her champions, Paul 1, on succeeding to the throne, issues an ukase prohibiting the spoken word.

Realizing that he must take a firm line with these rebels now or never, Paul issues a second ukase forbidding thought.

He enforces this ukase in no uncertain manner.

The following day, finding themselves thinking, some of his subjects seek to allay their fears by attending to their horses.

But if it is forbidden to speak, it is always possible to use sign-language.

This reign of terror gives the country a most singular appearance.

The terror becomes so widespread that Paul himself is affected by it, and it is well known how closely fear resembles that other disease of tsars. Within a few hours Paul succumbs.

This frightful regime of intimidation makes the Russians so base and cringing that even their bearing reveals it.

Fortunately this unbending tyrant is succeeded by a generous and high-minded prince, Alexander, who swiftly rouses his new subjects from the state of prostration in which they have been left by Paul.

But, perceiving with sorrow that baseness is ingrained in the Russian character, this high-minded prince sheds tears of warm-hearted contempt over his people.

Fortunately, however, he discovers in his huge empire several writers of a liberal persuasion whom he swiftly raises to the highest rank.

Alexander shows these simple-minded theorists, whose writings have been adopted to the letter by some people, that action is followed by reaction.

Even so, the stern measures that he is obliged to take, against his will, cause him great distress.

A HISTORY OF HOLY RUSSIA

His hatred of bloodshed leads this high-minded prince to abolish the death penalty, substituting the life penalty for it. This is a great disappointment to his intelligent subjects.

In his never-ending pursuit of humanitarian ends and in his efforts to alleviate human hardships, this warm-hearted prince finds a means of ensuring that his Siberian convicts never again return from exile frozen stiff.

But one thing, one thing alone, never ceases to torment the philosophical autocrat: that war can still be possible in this age of culture and brotherly love, to which the dread instruments still permitted to exist bear witness.

So, in his noble zeal to endow the world with a universal and lasting peace, he assembles all the kings of Europe and proposes that the territory of each nation be regarded henceforth as inviolable, under all circumstances, except in the inconceivable case of an attack on orthodoxy, though orthodoxy of course exists only in Russia and Russia no longer desires war. Furthermore, he proposes that the onerous but noble charge of punishing all those seeking to infringe the treaty be conferred upon him, the strongest amongst them.

Some more precise souls, suspecting that the "charge" which he sought might not be exactly amusing, ask for a closer definition of the terms of the treaty.

1812.

A HISTORY OF HOLY RUSSIA

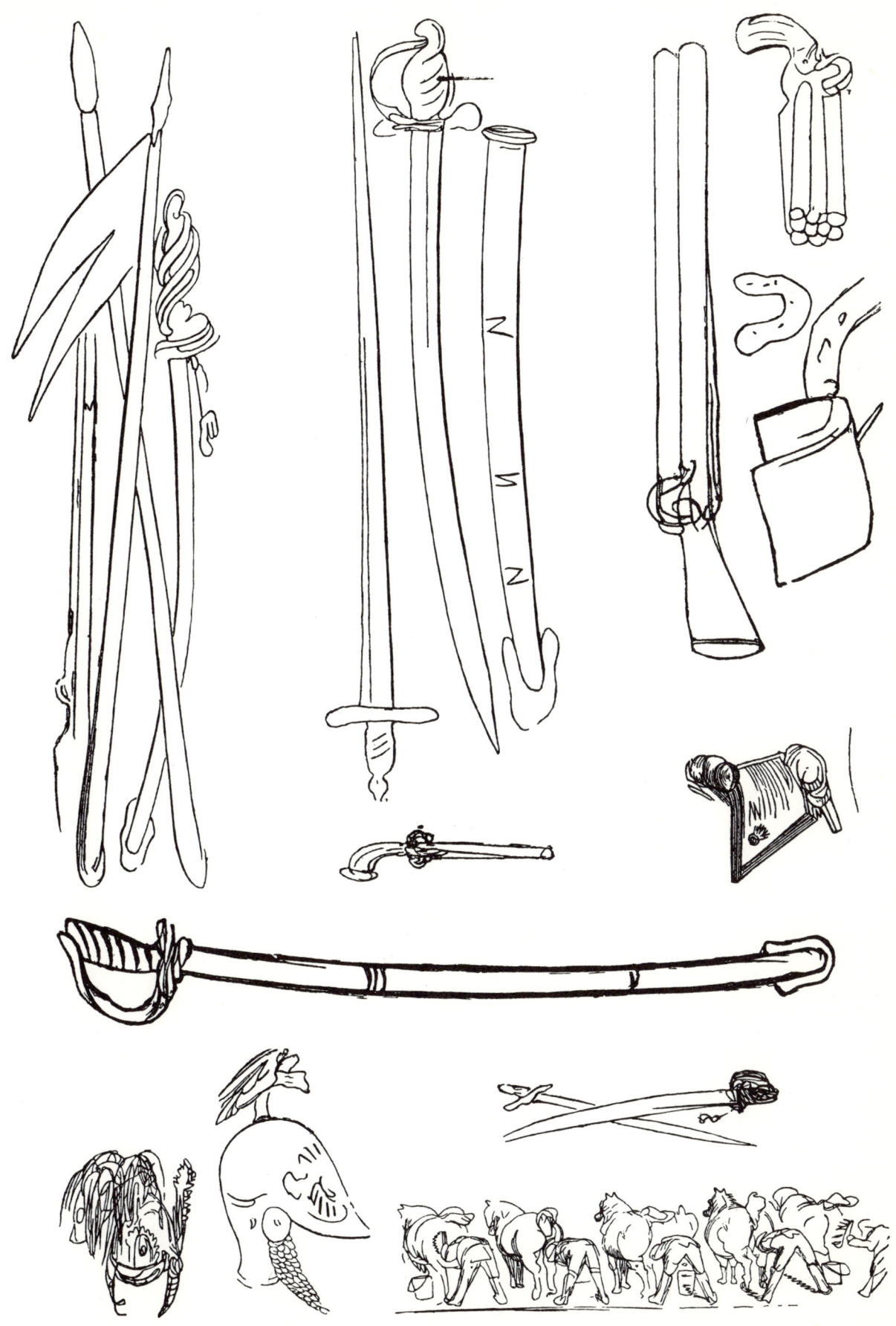

Accession of Nicholas I and the Reorganization of the Army.

A HISTORY OF HOLY RUSSIA

Establishment of a council whose members are under no obligation to give any.

Establishment of a society for promoting cattle-breeding under the patronage of His Imperial Majesty. The official prize-giving ceremony.

1828-1832
The yellow cuirass without a sun is replaced by the yellow and silver cuirass with a sun in the center.

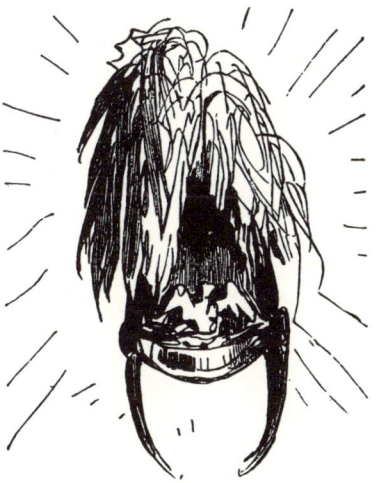

1832-1836
The upright, pale-yellow plume is replaced by the drooping, blue, red and green plume.

A HISTORY OF HOLY RUSSIA

Grand Ball at the Russian Court
Where the already widespread view that the Emperor, an exceptionally handsome man, stands head and shoulders above his subjects, is confirmed.

Some French actors engaged by the Petersburg court theatre are much surprised to discover that the part they are mostly called upon to perform is that of spectator.

Sober-minded people that they are, the Russians pride themselves on welcoming only experienced actors: they also insist their petite neighbors should take care to ripen *their* talents.

to the point where they need only be provided for.

Return to France of the above dancer whose resources substantially increased.

A HISTORY OF HOLY RUSSIA

The court of assizes at Kronstadt, *i.e.* the passport and visa office.

Another position that must frequently be adopted while waiting for the passport to be checked, in which it becomes clear that permission to enter hangs by a thread.

After this there remains only a careful sounding of one's opinions.

A recent arrival in Russia discovers, as M. Custine did, that in Petersburg even the walls have ears.

Foreign nobleman with friends in high places who has managed to secure the Tsar's permission for him to visit the national museums.

A HISTORY OF HOLY RUSSIA

Demeanor of the St. Petersburg populace now that the Emperor Nicholas' police organization is so highly respected.

A Russian subject charged with liberalism is suspected, investigated, tried and sentenced.

Oh dear! Oh dear! ... I feel I would like to place myself under police supervision.

Russian police head-quarters.

A HISTORY OF HOLY RUSSIA

The skaters of Lake Ladoga.

Anniversary of the victory of Austerlitz.

Sketch made at the frontier of all the Russias.

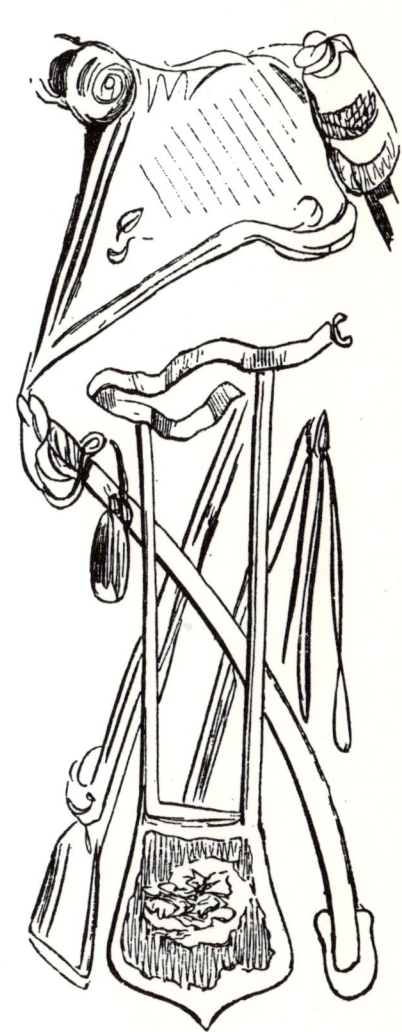

A HISTORY OF HOLY RUSSIA

147

The great Orthodox salad, decennial rite of the Greco-Russian church.

Faith,

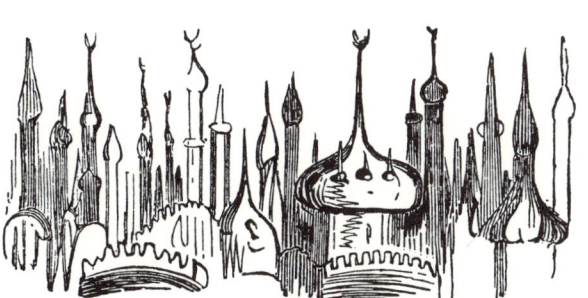

hope

and charity Orthodox-style.

On one salad day, Tsar Nicholas, rummaging among the piles of old and new testaments in the salad-bowl, discovers one even more recent, written by the hand of the Apostle Peter himself, and blushes when he realizes that he had forgotten he was appointed executor.

The ideas that flood his mind at this unexpected discovery immediately make him bald with ambition.

After which he wonders how to put his great schemes into operation as swiftly as possible. But in view of the meekness of his people, he fears that it will be hard to make heroes and conquerors of them. However, a moment later the Orthodox God speaks to him saying that one is low only if one seeks to be.

A HISTORY OF HOLY RUSSIA

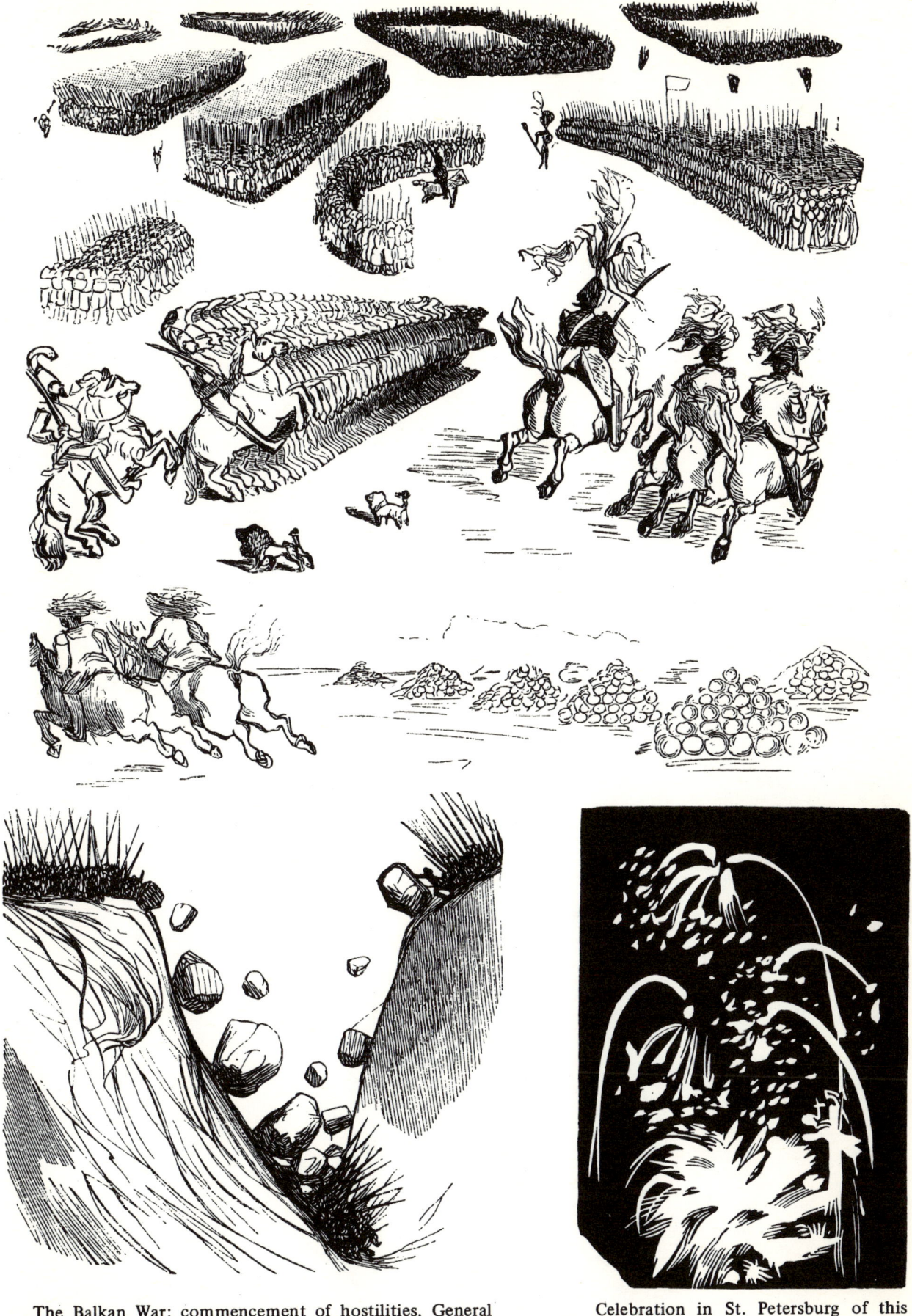

The Balkan War: commencement of hostilities. General Osten-Sacken informs H.M. the Emperor that, apart from a number of mishaps due to landfalls, the holy army has begun with some overwhelming victories.

Celebration in St. Petersburg of this overwhelming victory.

A HISTORY OF HOLY RUSSIA

Gamble follows gamble. Playing cards becomes a wild craze among the nobles and instantly spreads to all corners of the realm.

Soon, appreciating the correctness of the motto of Robert the Devil, the Russian lords change their stakes, betting first their landed property and then their human property.

Some serfs who have been lost in a game seek out their new master, who unfortunately has suffered a sudden reversal of fortune and has been stripped of everything.

As a result of a sudden gust of wind, these good folk are, for the first time, presented with the woeful spectacle of a noble in a state of nature, which thoroughly confuses them.

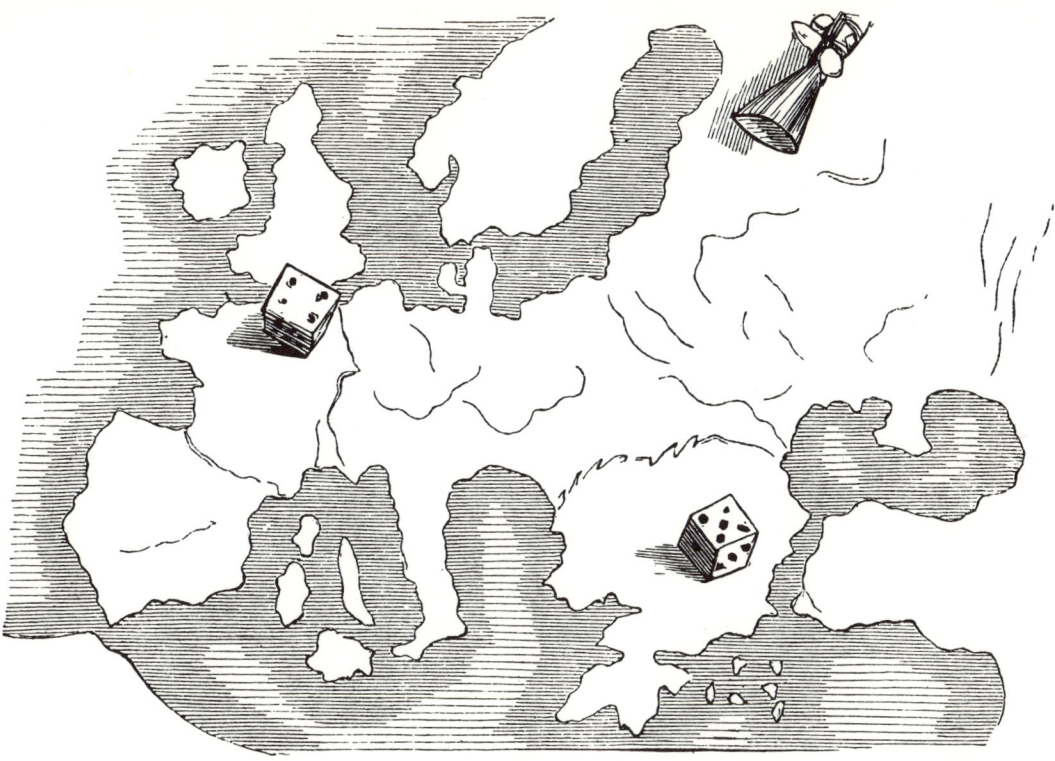

The mad craze for gambling spreads to the court, where the autocrat himself succumbs to it. The first stake he places does him full justice.

A peaceful Turkish peasant tries to make out the significance of the enigmatic object that has just landed in his field, and decides to refer the matter to His Majesty the Sultan.

An identical aerolith has just landed athwart the channel, one side resting on England and the other on France. The two nations, both of whose coasts have been damaged by this projectile, agree to furnish equal numbers of men to dispose of it at sea.

Meanwhile, Russian emissaries arrive to reclaim the object from the peasant who can only say that he is too weak to move it, adding however that he is expecting help from his friends.

But let us drop this tedious, allegorical manner which is, in any case, inappropriate in a work of history, adopting instead a simple narrative style to describe those events which have just led to war in Europe.

It was a fine May morning. The heavens were cloudless and a gentle breeze was blowing. A dazzling sun had risen over the Black Sea.

The Turkish population was that day celebrating the most joyous and most resplendent festival of the year.

A HISTORY OF HOLY RUSSIA

That same evening, as may be imagined, a great banquet is held at court. It is a splendid feast and there is much laughter and merry-making.

When dinner is over, Prince Menshikov, who has been one of the brightest and most animated of the guests, approaches H.M. the Sultan, draws him aside, and addresses him in the following manner:

"My dear sir, I had intended sharing a little secret, I might almost say a little surprise, with you over dessert, but uncertainty about my fellow guests and the tremendous uproar of the thousand-and-one-conversations made me put it off till the present moment.

"You must be aware, my dear sir, that Russia has at all times been able to maintain 1,200,000 under arms and to raise a further 2,000,000 if necessary. This army, a kind of European police force or judicial executive, as it were, has never wavered in its duty of safeguarding the peace whenever it is threatened in the country of one of our weaker neighbors. At the first call for aid from one of *these gentlemen,* His Imperial Majesty has always made all possible haste to visit upon the foolhardy rebels the full wrath of his autocratic person. But he is even more kindly disposed toward you, sir, whom he has always honored and still honors with his special friendship and whom he has always clearly favored . . . Others, in order to obtain generous subsidies from him (as you may have seen for yourself in recent years) have had to ask for them. But your wishes, sir, he has anticipated, desiring to spare you the embarrassment, as a proud Sultan, of having to entreat him. Therefore, believe it or not, 200,000 men are already encamped on the frontier of your empire, ready to cross the Prut and to restore order (with your help, which would only be right) between our turbulent co-religionists and your impetuous and intolerant disciples of Mahomet. What say you sir? Is that not good breeding, is that not loving you well and showering you with favors . . .?"

"By heavens, sir, only grooms or *parvenus* adopt so familiar a tone with each other, and if you commit this indiscretion again, I shall ask you to take your leave."

"I would rather take the Porte—and, to be frank, it is only Russian courtesy that has obliged me to address you in this roundabout manner. A peasant like yourself, who takes offence when a good friend speaks to him in a familiar manner, should not be treated with kid gloves, and a Russian nobleman will not hesitate to speak his mind if he is gratuitously insulted. Yes, sir, at first we were reluctant to inform you that your Mahometan subjects were rascals, vagabonds, good-for-nothings, in a word, Turks. It was not easy to say all that to you. Moreover, acting on a generous impulse, we went so far as to accuse our own co-religionists of contributing to the disturbances. However, with someone as indiscreet as yourself, there is nothing for it but to speak openly.

"Long enough have our noble brothers in Orthodoxy endured the savage disregard of your cruel Koran-worshippers, not to mention the continual offence caused by the multiplicity of their wives. Furthermore, your city is full of unmuzzled dogs which strike terror into them, a fact that you have consistently ignored. When you spoke that fine and noble word *hospitality,* you were surely aware that to offer someone hospitality is to tell him to *make himself at home.* Now, are our subjects at home in Turkey or in Constantinople, or are they not? . . . Clearly they are not. I shall not speak here of those straits whose narrowness is a permanent impediment, a perpetual challenge, as it were, to our maritime freedom. This could not have been endured for so long, sir, but for the extraordinary forebearance of our magnanimous Emperor, but since you, sir, have had the audacity to break the ice, we shall boldy state our grievances and not hesitate to inform you that all these affronts demand a revenge worthy of the warriors of 1812 . . . My dear sir, it is sheer stubbornness on your part to insist on ruling here. It is insolent mockery of my master's authority. As matters stand now, only your abdication in favor of the Tsar, my master, can make amends; you must decide on your course of action by tomorrow. I, for my part, must leave you now. I see that it is ten o'clock and I have guests this evening. Think it over and come to see me tomorrow or the day after. I bid you good night."

A HISTORY OF HOLY RUSSIA

Several long and painful days having elapsed without H.M. the Sultan paying His Excellency a visit to apologize, as best he might, for his discourtesy, Prince Menshikov himself visits Abdul and, leaving his Muscovite pride and arrogance at the palace gates, so as better to be able to fulfil his role of diplomat and conciliator, he says upon entering:

"My dear sir, I shall make one last attempt to avert the European crisis that your fatal stubbornness is bringing to a head. Once again I ask you to allow us to govern your country and all will be forgotten. The blessings of peace will be restored to the world and everything will flourish again in the fertile breath of universal tranquillity. If, on the other hand, in your ignorance and folly, you decide upon a different course, what shall be the result? War with all its horrors! War!! A harsh word and one I thought my lips had forgotten how to utter. War!!! Do you know what that means, sir? Rivers overflowing with blood; the poor man's cottage burnt to the ground; a marriage of hunch-backs! War . . . means the end of all love and charity. It is the barbarians' revenge on civilization. It is the hatred of absolute strangers for each other. It is a return to the past. It is madness, frenzy, ignorance. It is the old Europe savagely rending the new. For pity's sake, think of the blood that will be shed, and what blood? The flower of our land and of yours. Treacherous friends or some late-comers to civilization are leading you astray, either out of malice or stupidity. Do you not realize that when France and England, those two perfidious nations, speak of honor, fair play and peace, they are simply camouflaging their plan to enforce the treaties of the old, bellicose Europe and to protect themselves against our righteous covetousness?

"You speak of integrity! Would it be betraying your principles to accept the post offered you by my generous master?" "Enough, sir," answers Abdul, "you should *not use* such words." "*If not you*, then it must be your brother, or some member of your household. Oh, forgive me, what am I saying? I am growing confused, and . . ." "Not at all, not at all, on the contrary, I have always acknowledged the Russian talent for mimicry. Only, if you think you will fleece me, I must point out that my *bristles are up*. Finally, since you are evidently so determined to take your leave as well as our Porte, I must beg you to do the first at once and I shall even provide two footmen to assist you in case you are uncertain as to the procedure."

The prince, in transports of joy at this warm suggestion, returns to the capital of his own country.

A HISTORY OF HOLY RUSSIA

Prince Menshikov's return to St. Petersburg.

How some statesmen of Nicholas, by hare-brain'd counsel, put him in extreme danger.

(F. Rabelais, *History of Russia and of Nicholas the most dread and terrifying son of Grandgousier,* Book 1, ch. XXXIII.)

... There came before Nicholas the Duke of Smalltrash, the Earle Swash-buckler, and Captain Durtaille, who said unto him, Sir, this day we make you the happiest, the most warlike and chivalrous Prince that ever was since the death of Alexander of Macedonia. Be covered, be covered, (said Nicholas.) Grammercie (said they) we do but our duty: The manner is thus, you shall leave some Captain here to have the charge of this Garrison, with a Party competent for keeping of the place, which besides its natural strength, is made stronger by the rampiers and fortresses of your devising. Your Army you are to divide into two parts, as you know very well how to do. One part thereof shall fall upon Abdul Medjid and his forces, by it shall he be easily at the very first shock routed, and then shall you get money by heaps, for the Clown hath store of ready coine: Clown we call him, because a noble and generous Prince hath never a penny and that to hoard up treasure is but a clownish trick.

The other part of the Army in the mean time shall draw towards Onys, Xaintonge, Angoulesme and Gascony: then march to Perigourt, Medos, and Elanes, taking wherever you come without resistance, townes, castles, and forts: Afterwards to Bayonne, St. John de Luz, to Fuéntarabia, where you shall seize upon all the ships, and coasting along Galicia and Portugal, shall pillage all the maritime places, even unto Lisbone, where you shall be supplied with all necessaries befitting a Conquerour. By copsodie Spain will yield, for they are but a race of Loobies: then are you to passe by the streights of Gibralter, where you shall erect two pillars more stately than those of Hercules, to the perpetual memory of your name, and the narrow entrance there shall be called the Nicholine sea.

Having past the Nicholine sea, behold Barbarossa yields himself your slave: I will (said Nicholas) give him faire quarter and spare his life. Yes (said they) so that he be content to be christened. And you shall conquer the Kingdomes of Tunes, of Hippos, Argier, Bomine, Corode, yea all Barbary. Furthermore, you shall take into your hands Majorca, Minorca, Sardinia, Corsica, with the other Islands of the Ligustick and Balearian seas. Going alongst on the left hand, you shall rule all Gallia Narbonensis, Provense, the Allobrogians, Genua, Florence, Luca, and then by God's leave Rome; The poor Pope has already died. By my faith (said Nicholas) I will not then kisse his pantuffle.

Italy being thus taken, behold, Naples, Calabria, Apulia and Sicilie all ransacked, and Malta too. I wish the pleasant Knights of the Rhodes heretofore would but come to resist you, that we might see their urine. I would (said Nicholas) very willingly go to Loretta. No, no, (said they) that shall be at our return; from thence we will saile Eastwards, and take Candia, Cyprus, Rhodes, and the Cyclade Islands, and set upon Morea. It is ours by St. Trenian, the Lord preserve Jerusalem; for the great Soldan is not comparable to you in power. I will then (said he) cause Solomon's Temple to be built. No, (said they) not yet, have a little patience, stay a while, be never too sudden in your enterprises.

Can you tell what Octavian Augustus said? *Festina lente*, It is requisite that you first have the lesser Asia, Caria, Lycia, Pamphilia, Cilicia, Lydia, Phrygia, Mysia, Bithynia, even unto Euphrates. Shall we see (said Nicholas) Babylon and Mount Sinai? There is no need (said they) at this time; have we not hurried up and down, travelled and toyled enough, in having transfreted and past over the Hircanian sea, marched alongst the two Armenias and the three Arabias? By my faith (said he) we have played the fooles, and are undone; Ha, poor soules! What's the matter, said they? What shall we have (said he) to drink in these deserts? For Julian Augustus, with his whole Army died there for thirst, as they say. We have already (said they), given order for that. In the Siriack sea you have nine thousand and fourteen great ships laden with the best wines in the world: they arrived at Port Joppa, there they found two and twenty thousand Camels, and sixteen hundred Elephants, which you shall have taken at one hunting about Sigelmes, when you entered into Lybia: and, besides this, you had all the Mecca Caravane. Did not they furnish you sufficiently with wine? Yes, but (said he) we did not drink it fresh. By the vertue, (said they) not of a fish, a valiant man, a Conquerour, who pretends and aspires to the Monarchy of the world, cannot alwayes have this ease. God be thanked, that you and your men are come safe and sound unto the banks of the river Tigris.

But (said he) what doth that part of our Army in the mean time, which overthrows that unworthy Swill-pot Abdul? They are not idle (said they) we shall meet with them by and by, they shall have won you Britany, Normandy, Flanders, Haynault, Brabant, Artois, Holland, Zealand; they have past the Rhine over the bellies of the Switsers and Lanskenets, and a Party of these hath subdued Luxemburg, Lorrain, Champaigne, and Savoy, even to Lions, in which place they have met with your forces, returning from the naval Conquests of the Mediterranean sea: and have rallied again in Bohemia, after they had plundered and sacked Suevia, Wittemberg, Bavaria, Austria, Moravia, and Styria. Then they set fiercely together upon Lubeck, Norway, Swedeland, Rie, Denmark, Gitland, Greenland, the Sterlins, even unto the frozen sea: this done, they conquered the iles of Orkney, and subdued Scotland, England, and Ireland. From thence sailing through the sandie sea, and by the Sarmates, they have vanquished and overcome Prussia, Poland, Lituania, Russia, Walachia, Transilvania, Hungarie, Bulgaria, Turquieland, and are now at Constantinople.

Come (said Nicholas), let us go joyn with them quickly, for I will be Emperour of Trebezonde also: shall we not kill all these dogs, Turks and Mahumetans? What a devil should we do else, said they: and you shall give their goods and lands to such as shall have served you honestly. Reason (said he) will have it so, that is but just, I give unto you the Caramania, Surie, and all the Palestine. Ha, Sir, (said they) it is out of your goodnesse: Grammercie, we thank you, God grant you may alwayes prosper.

There was there present at that time an old Gentleman well experienced in the warres, a sterne souldier, and who had been in many hazards, named Echephron, who hearing this discourse, said, I do greatly doubt that all this enterprise will be like the tale or interlude of the pitcher full of milk, wherewith a Shoemaker made himself

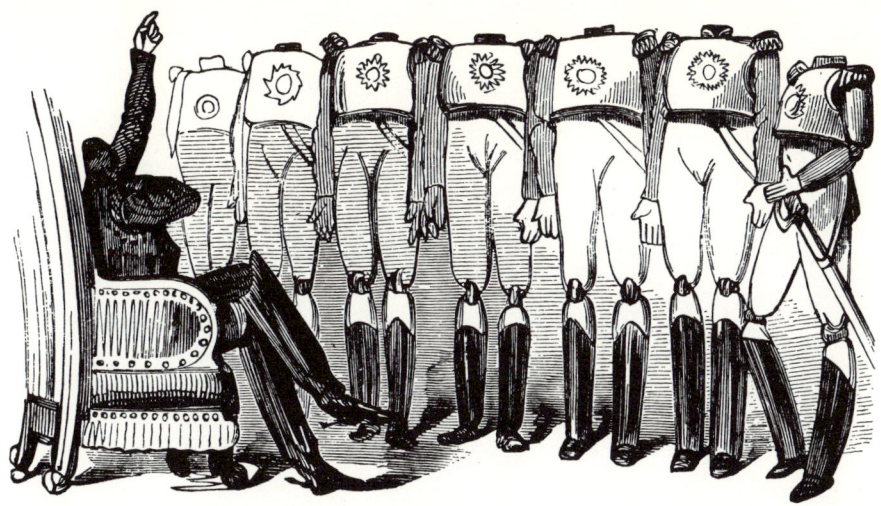

rich in conceit: but, when the pitcher was broken, he had not whereupon to dine: what do you pretend by these large Conquests? what shall be the end of so many labours and crosses? Thus it shall be (said Nicholas) that when we are returned, we shall sit down, rest and be merry. But (said Echephron), if by chance you should never come back, for the voyage is long and dangerous, were it not better for us to take our rest now, then unnecessarily to expose our selves to so many dangers? O (said Swashbuckler,) by G--, here is a good dotard, come, let us go hide our selves in the corner of a chimney, and there spend the whole time of our life amongst ladies, in threading of pearles, or spinning like Sardanapalus: He that nothing ventures, hath neither horse nor mule, (sayes Solomon). He who adventureth too much (said Echephron) loseth both horse and mule, answered Malchon. Enough (said Nicholas,) go forward: I fear nothing but that these devillish legions of Napoleon, whilest we are in Mesopotamia, will come on our backs, and charge up our reer, what course shall we then take? what shall be our remedy? A very good one (said Durtaille), a pretty little commission, which you must send unto the Muscoviters, shall bring you into the field in an instant foure hundred and fifty thousand choice men of warre. O that you would but make me your Lieutenant General, I should for the lightest faults of any inflict great punishments. I charge, I strike, I take, I kill, I slay, I play the devil. On, on, (said Nicholas) make haste, my lads, and let him that loves me, follow me.

The following day the Emperor Nicholas, Tsar of all the Russias, King of all the Polands, Emperor of all the Siberias, autocrat of the whole bag-of-tricks (glory be to God and to the most Holy Orthodox Church), assembles the Imperial guard and addresses them solemnly:

"Crusaders!!! I have called you here to inform you that the time has at last come for us to show our true face to Europe. It will soon be 44 years since any of the nations of this continent have followed the honorable paths of war. It is both shrewd and pertinent to seek fame and glory at a time when all the nations of Europe are in decline, when peace has so weakened them, so depraved them, that they have forgotten the glory war brings. Rise! And may Europe fall at the very sight of you!

"But let me address you in Latin, as befits an Orthodox Tsar, for it will be both more venerable and more inspiring.

NICOLAUS NOBISCUM! QUIS CONTRA NOS?...

Ut inimicos sanctae Ecclesiae humiliare digneris, te rogamus, audi nos; ut regibus et principibus christianis pacem et veram concordiam donare digneris; ut cuncto populo christiano pacem et unitatem largiri digneris, te rogamus, audi nos. Esto nobis, domine, turris fortitudinis a facie inimici. Aamen. The time has passed, young heroes, when men fought for their countries; some countries of Europe are still, I know, at that stage, but therein lies our advantage. You should fight under the sole banner of *Tsar and Glory*; listen to the words of the prophetic angel: *Mandavit Deus nubibus desuper, et januas coeli aperuit, et pluit illis, etc. Alleluia: Ps.: 'Attendite populi mei, legem meam; inclinate aurem vestram in verba oris mei. Gloria patri, etc.* Give no thought to the possibility of defeat; we shall not be defeated, for the God of battle is upon our side: *Si fractus illabatur orbis, impavidum ferient ruinae.* Chastise the infidel who would substitute a degenerate order for war, that goddess of the Old Testament! Show these men who doubt your strength that you are still the savage barbarians of 1812! The sun of Austerlitz, where, as you know, you conquered, shall shine once again upon you. *Nicolaus et Deus vobis cum; quis contra vos?* Take this standard, and remember the motto upon it: *in hoc signo vinces.* One word more: I know that you are invincible; it is therefore unnecessary to remind you of the glorious year 1812. However, if your courage fails you (which it will not), may this date be your battle cry: 1812!! ... 1812!! ... 1812!! ... *Lapides clamabunt.* You need no longer try to hold back your enthusiasm. I particularly commend to your attention the perfidious French who in an underhand manner civilize and reconcile all things. People who have the audacity to publish private correspondence should not be given any quarter: and besides, Paris is beautiful and Paris is large, London is wealthy, Constantinople is enchanting, and God is infinite in his goodness and mercy. *Gloria Patri,* etc. Upon you I bestow the honor of planting the flag of Russia in all the capitals of pagan and barbarian Europe: 1812!! ... 1812!! ... At the very sound of it, my pulse races! My good 1812, my sweet 1812!! my darling; upon my word, I weep, *et ecce lacrymabar!!!* 1812, 1812, 1812, 1812, my honor, 1812!! my salvation! *Domine, Domine! ad te clamavi,* 1812. *Tityre tu patulae recubans sub tegmine,* etc., etc. Go, and may the true faith guide you! 1812!! you will be victorious and will safeguard the future of your ancestors!!! Amen!"

A HISTORY OF HOLY RUSSIA

Council held to determine the best means of taking Odessa.

The hornets and the bees.

A HISTORY OF HOLY RUSSIA

(To the tune of " The good King Dagobert ")

Trying to see the light of day
The Tsar looked through his spy glass the wrong way.
One of his boyars
Said to him: O Tsar,
Your Majesty
Won't be able to see.
Not so, he replied.
The wrong end's the right.

Good king Nicholas
Declared himself weary of peace.
One of his boyars
Said to him: Oh Tsar,
Your Majesty
Has lost his way.
Maybe, the king replied.
But Peter was even more mystified.

Good King Nicholas
He pursued a downward course.
One of his boyars
Said to him: O Tsar,
Soon you'll be found
Flat on the ground.
'Tis so, came the king's rejoinder.
Bit by bit we shall founder.

A HISTORY OF HOLY RUSSIA

Good king Nicholas
Dreamt of Attila, no less.
One of his boyars
Said to him: Oh Tsar,
The role of Hun
Is no longer fun.
Not so, said Nicholas.
Is a Tsar less conspicuous?

Good king Nicholas
Longed for the sun's caress.
One of his boyars
Said to him: Oh Tsar,
Your Majesty
Will sweat mightily.
'Tis so, said the king.
Burning is no worse than freezing.

Good King Nicholas
Left Lake Ladoga's shores.
One of his boyars
Said to him: Oh Tsar,
Your Majesty's
Head is turned, I see.
'Tis so, Nicholas riposted.
But you'll not turn me from it.

Good King Nicholas
Made Orthodoxy ridiculous.
One of his boyars
Said to him: Oh Tsar,
You masquerade as
An ancient crusader.
'Tis so, Nicholas replies.
But none will see through my disguise.

Good King Nicholas
Kept burbling protectorate.
One of his boyars
Said to him: Oh Tsar,
These good Christians all
Feel perfectly well.
Not so, said the king.
And I'll prove it ere long.

Good King Nicholas
Liked to make himself conspicuous.
One of his boyars
Said to him: Oh Tsar,

All they understand
Is an iron hand.
'Tis so, said that satrap.
And I'll combine it with the strap.

A HISTORY OF HOLY RUSSIA

Good King Nicholas
Wanted to shell Kronstadt(1)
One of his boyars
Said to him: Oh Tsar,
At the first broadside
It'll fall on its side.
Said the Tsar, so much the better.
If it falls it'll block the Neva.

Nicholas the good Tsar
Awaited fresh strength from the Shah.
One of his boyars
Said to him: Oh Tsar,
I think that this Shah's
Got a fine set of claws.
Rubbish, Nicholas spat,
Do you think the Shah's a cat!

Good King Nicholas
Had his eye on Odessa.
One of his boyars
Said to him: Oh Tsar,

Your Majesty's
Scarce fortified.
Good, Nicholas replied.
Then we'll see some heroic deeds.

(1) My apologies for this rhyme [and others too: Translator's note]. I feel that a few such imperfections are permissible here, particularly as there is clearly neither rhyme nor reason in Russia.

A HISTORY OF HOLY RUSSIA

Good Tsar Nicholas
Had all his decks cleared for action.
One of his boyars
Said to him: Oh Tsar,
You will surely go
To the bottom (oh!).
Never mind, said the emperor.
Others have gone there before.

Good Tsar Nicholas
Dreamt of Admiral Dundas.
One of his boyars
Said to him: Oh Tsar,
This rear-admiral
Will not do you well.
'Tis so, said Nicholas.
But *Osten* is not propitious.

Good King Nicholas
Much deplored this ballywrack.
One of his boyars
Said to him: Oh Tsar,
From Sinop I foretell
That all will not be well.
'Tis so, said that ruler.
But still, I thought they were too civilized and too indolent to get there.

A HISTORY OF HOLY RUSSIA

Good King Nicholas
Not so firmly allied thought us;
One of his boyars
Said to him: Oh Tsar,
Your Majesty
Is wrong, you see.
'Tis so, said Nicholas aloud.
I thought the allies would fall out.

Good King Nicholas.
Declared it would not last.
One of his boyars
Said to him: Oh Tsar,
Lady Birch'em
Runs the kitchen.
Maybe, said the king.
But this is no time for joking.

Good Tsar Nicholas
Saw France quickening its pace.
One of his boyars
Said to him: Oh Tsar,

Against that a Cossack
Is just an old hack.
'Tis so, the king said.
But Napoleon said it before you did.

Good King Nicholas
Wanted to get out of the impasse.
One of his boyars
Said to him: Oh Tsar,

Your Majesty
Has come to far.
'Tis so, said that potentate.
And I fear I have left it too late.

However, taken aback by this onset of humility, the haughty Tsar thinks better of it, and lifting his proud head he smashes a bottle at the feet of the pusillanimous boyar to emphasize his point that the West will not be able to offer him any resistance.

The obstinate boyar remains unconvinced, and the forceful Tsar makes his point even more abundantly clear by squashing a fly on the window pane.

He then conducts the judicious and skeptical boyar before his army, impressing him with its invincible appearance and forcing him to admit, besides, how accurate is the comparison made between it and a musical score.

"Even so," says the tedious boyar, "this score, as I see it, contains but one rest amongst much quavering..."

From there he takes him to the armory to show him how heavy are his cannonballs.

But the tedious boyar retorts that the last cannon-ball to strike home will be of somewhat larger dimensions.

Deeply impressed by the wisdom of this reply, the Emperor suddenly forms the highest opinion of his councillor's intelligence and decides to appoint him chief superintendent of the Siberian mines.

The Emperor Nicholas I's death certificate.

Nevertheless, he awards him the cross of St. Andrew to cheer him on his way. The philosophical gentleman, who understands the true nature of Orthodoxy better than his Tsar, takes comfort in the knowledge that each man must bear his cross in this world.

A HISTORY OF HOLY RUSSIA

Certain cosmopolitans of progressive outlook reproach Napoleon III for embarking on so risky a war.

But others, less cosmopolitan perhaps, though clearly even more progressive, have, indeed, already got as far as Varna, where they await the coming trials, passing the time in the meanwhile by imagining a future full of Glory and, above all, Honor.

Moral and Epilogue

If thy house must come to ruine, should it therefore in its fall crush the heels of him that set it up? The matter is so unreasonable, and so dissonant from common sense, that hardly can it be conceived by humane understanding, and altogether incredible unto strangers, till by the certain and undoubted effects thereof it be made apparent, that nothing is either sacred or holy to those, who having emancipated themselves from God and reason, do merely follow the perverse, *or should we say orthodox,* affections of their own depraved nature.

(F. Rabelais, *History of Russia* or *The Life of Gargantua*)

". . . It's like I said, if our lads manage to give their Tsar a thrashing, we'll lay it on hard like they was beasts. After that we'll make it up and be friends!!!" (Achille Champavert, Corporal in the 23rd Infantry regiment)

A HISTORY OF HOLY RUSSIA

The North Star.

A HISTORY OF HOLY RUSSIA

You are disturbing it, said this cruel creature. (La Fontaine)

The Jack-in-the-box.

A HISTORY OF HOLY RUSSIA

Lord, how misleading most proverbs are! Think of it: to demand the impossible is to cry for the moon! Well, we'll see about that.

A HISTORY OF HOLY RUSSIA

How the Russians aspire to all that is well-established.

A Russian spy attending a performance of *The Cossacks,* wonders at the manner in which the *gods* regard his master's orthodoxy.

You fool, Champavert! Big fellows like that are never strong, they die young.

If he always moves backwards, he'll never see the dangers lurking behind him.

A HISTORY OF HOLY RUSSIA

The chief aim of the Russians.—The greasy pole is taller even than the highest peaks of the Urals. In spite of the considerable experience they have had in such slippery matters, they try in vain to reach the light. Melting oil flows over the reckless Muscovites. The autocratic flittermouse alone manages to reach the flame, but the heat there is too great and the nocturnal creature burns its wings. The other participants slide and slither over each other and are in danger of melting into the fat (when they would rather have absorbed it into themselves.)

A HISTORY OF HOLY RUSSIA

Russia's annual cure carried out by Doctor Schamyl: fifty Caucasian leeches applied each autumn.

A HISTORY OF HOLY RUSSIA

The Danubian mist or the Muscovite nightmare.

A HISTORY OF HOLY RUSSIA

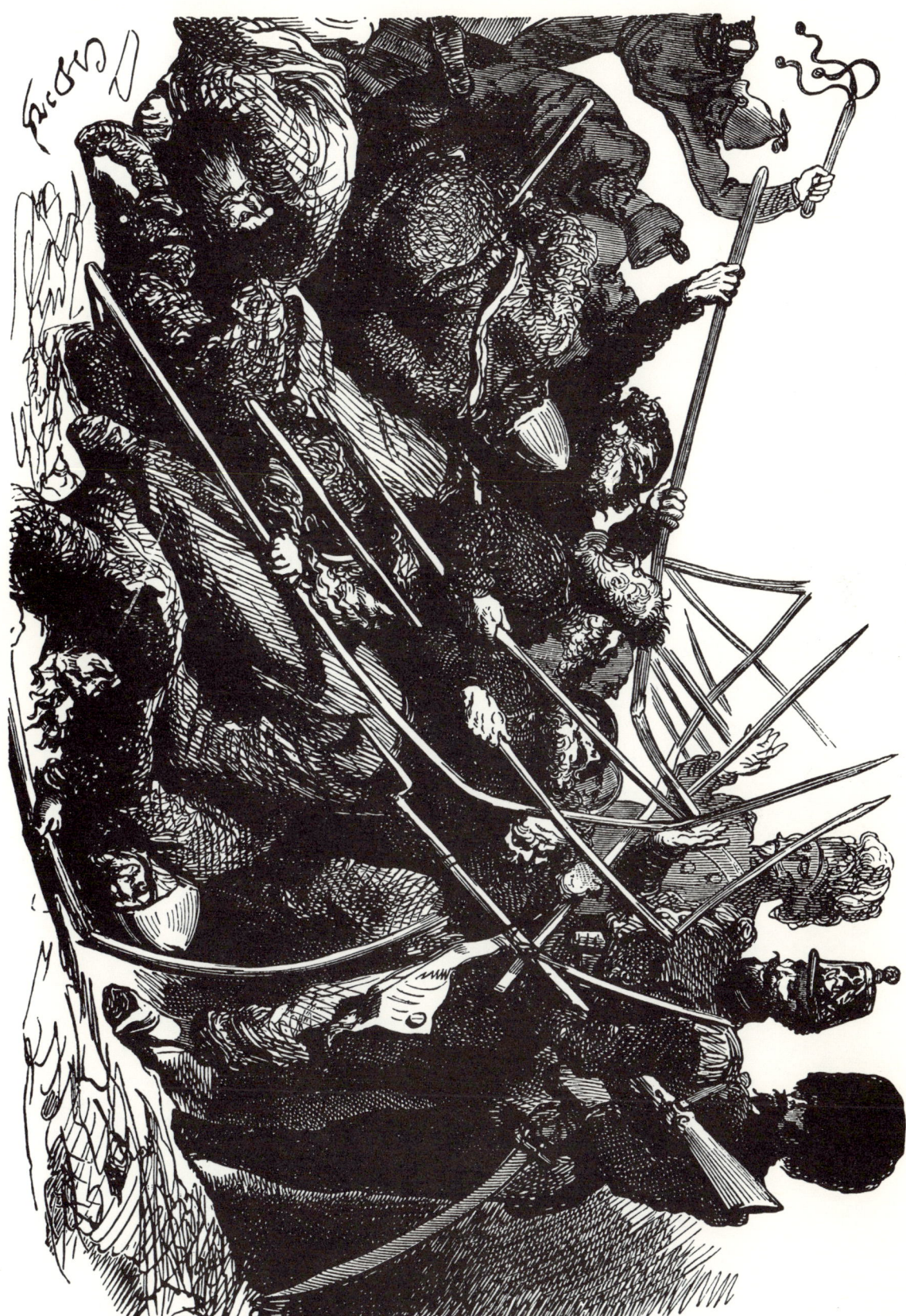

The Soldiers of Peace
Let us spare these poor wretches,
Who reluctantly bear arms against us.

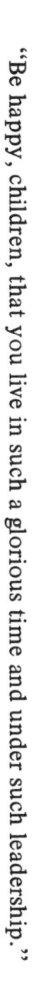

1854 encountering 1812
"Be happy, children, that you live in such a glorious time and under such leadership."

"You've been mumbling 1812 between your teeth long enough, old chap, now you can stuff it down your gullet..."

A HISTORY OF HOLY RUSSIA

"Well Champavert, forty Russian ships and two hundred houses burnt. Is that enough for you?"

"All the same, it's a pity. If only there was some way of doing 'em in without hurting 'em!"

"Champavert, you're talking like an innocent . . . or maybe you've just been reading books . . . eh, Champavert?"

A HISTORY OF HOLY RUSSIA 207

"Patience Champavert! Patience! We'll get there in the end no need to be as bloodthirsty as all that about the Russians."

"Bloodthirsty yourself—can't you see that if we don't get there soon, we'll 'ave to kill too many of them fine fellows."

THE END

GUSTAVE DORÉ

ONE of the great graphic artists of the 19th century in France, Gustave Doré (1832-1883) is beginning to come into his own again. Several of his brilliantly illustrated books have recently been brought back into print, and now with this new edition of *The History of Holy Russia* we see how original and important he was—influencing artists all the way from Courbet (who once said, "There are only two of us!") to the popular David Levine of our own day.

Doré's famous illustrations to the Bible and to Dante, his sketches of London and Paris, have long been favorites among those who love an artist who has both a soaring imagination and a keen satirical eye for all the details of life around him. Doré's work, like Daumier's, combines both. This book, put together with a quite musical sense of rhythm, is full of unforgettable portraits and scenes—Doré, in a whirlwind, produced more than 500 woodcuts for it—and it will be an enthralling experience for readers interested in both history and art. (One can also detect here why Doré the cartoonist has been considered to be the "father of the comic strip.")

In his own life-time Doré became widely known for his illustrations to Dante's *Inferno* (1861), *Don Quixote* (1862), the Bible (1866) and *The Wandering Jew* (1866) and is generally recognized for his contribution in establishing the illustrated book of large format. Even in his best work, in his Rabelais and Münchausen albums, there is the romantic love of the grotesque; but his political interests and social emphases, so strong in this Russian work were also echoed later in his studies of London (only recently reprinted).

In a recent appreciation of Doré's work, the famous European critic, François Bondy, has called attention to the rhythmic impulse and the "musical variations," and has emphasized Doré's own musical education as a violinist and the influence of his brother Ernest who was a composer. In Bondy's phrase, Doré's *Histoire de la Sainte Russie* was "a score for the eye," with subtle and calculated changes of tone and tempo. "Indeed, this combination of a musical principal with a cabarettistic element make of Doré's achievement something more than simply caricature. The captions and the graphics hang together, not unlike the collaboration in Offenbach's operettas, only here Doré is his own librettist...."

The words themselves, as Professor Richard Pipes (of Harvard University) emphasized in the new introduction to this edition, have an importance and special interest. Beyond the puns and the obvious political tendentiousness (an anti-Russianism which Doré shared with most of his contemporaries, including Karl Marx), there is an imaginative range and power. François Bondy has pointed out that a German edition was published in the year 1917, but the omission of some twenty-three drawings distorted the character of the work. Professor Pipes sets Doré authoritatively in the whole context of the image-makers of the Russian character, from the Marquis de Custine to George F. Kennan.

This new facsimile edition of Doré's *History of Holy Russia* (for which Daniel Weissbort has done the first translation into English) is more than an intriguing and amusing curiosity, it is a work of permanent fascination.